D1523830

Quantitative Methods for Business

Patrick R. McMullen,

Wake Forest University
School of Business

This book is dedicated to the memory of Professor Ken Ramsing of the University of Oregon. Ken took a chance on me. I will always be grateful for that.

Contents

Introduction

The decision to write this book was made over time and eventually out of necessity. I have seen the students and their families spend too much money for their textbooks in addition to skyrocketing tuition costs. This problem didn't reach a critical point with me until my children became of college age, when I experienced the problem myself.

As such, I started on this book in September of 2015, so that the students can have a good reference to help them learn introductory business statistics while avoiding dependency on the large publishing companies and their outrageous prices.

Another reason for this book is so that there is more consistency between my lectures and the content in the book. One of the common bits of feedback from my students was that they didn't like the book – the expensive book from the publishing company, that is. I don't think the quality of the book was the problem, but the way I used the book was the problem. With this book, I am better able to coordinate my lectures with the book, which will benefit the students. There is stronger relationship between the book, the lectures, and the homework assignments.

The homework problems in the book refer to data sets which I have created, which will also result in better coordination between lectures and assignments.

Software

For this class, Microsoft Excel, version 2013 and later, is the software package of choice. While I do not consider Microsoft Excel the best statistics software available, it is the one software package to which essentially all students will have access. I liken Microsoft Excel's ability to perform statistics similar to a Swiss Army knife – it does a lot of things well, but no one thing exceptionally well. Microsoft Excel is flexible, and provides the tools for successful data analysis in a classroom setting.

Another software package used on occasion, is JMP, a general statistical software package made by SAS. JMP goes beyond the features of Microsoft with more ease than Excel. JMP is not used as often as Microsoft Excel because of the limited availability of JMP beyond the university years. Nevertheless, JMP is used on occasion to show some software capabilities that Excel simply cannot perform. This is especially the case when performing certain types of graphics.

Another software package used on rare occasion is "R." R is what is known as an "open-source" software package distributed by a group of users known as the "R-project." This means that R is freely downloadable, and the users can make enhancements to the software as they see fit. The software is frequently updated, and some of the new enhancements are included with new versions, assuming the new enhancements are deemed valuable by the leadership of the R-project. R is extremely powerful software, and can handle any type of problem we encounter in this class. The only downside associated with R is that it takes a little time to become familiar with its functionality. But after the basics are learned, R becomes very useful.

Data sets are available via www.joydivisionman.com/StatBooks

Course "Prerequisites"

For this course, a basic understanding of high-school or college algebra is a must. Beyond that, some "mathematical maturity" is needed at times. In statistics, we often sum quantities and we use subscript notation to do this. It is not to appear pretentious, but it is needed to explain something as briefly as possible.

As one reads this book, particularly when trying to understand the formulae, it is important to realize that this is not "bedtime reading." It takes time to digest the concepts explained. That is why examples are provided as deemed necessary.

The other prerequisite is that it is important to have a basic understanding of Microsoft Excel. By basic understanding, it is expected that the student is able to build a formula, copy and paste, and create basic charts.

New to This Edition

This edition is an aggregation of earlier editions, with the intent of providing coverage for a two-course sequence in quantitative methods. Additionally, some corrections have been made to the prior edition. Finally, more practice problems have been added to the end-of-chapter sections.

1. Why Statistics?

Statistics is a feared entity in the business school – for both undergraduate and MBA students. I personally fit this theory given that I received a grade of "D" when I first took statistics as an undergraduate engineering student. Assuming you've not thrown your book away over that revelation, I will continue. ☺

Prior to taking statistics for the first time, I was excited about the class. The reason for this, as embarrassing as it may be, was because I thought I already had a handle on what statistics was all about. As a schoolboy, my friends and I would trade baseball cards, in our effort to have a complete collection. If I had two 1974 cards of Pete Rose, but I was lacking a 1974 Henry Aaron card, I would gladly forfeit one of my Pete Rose cards for the Henry Aaron card.

Baseball cards are rife with statistics on the player's performance throughout their careers. In 1974, Henry Aaron broke the all-time home run record, held for a long time by baseball legend Babe Ruth. When Hank Aaron accomplished this seemingly impossible feat, he forever cemented himself as a legend of the game. Table 1.1 shows selected career hitting statistics for Henry Aaron.

Career	G	AB	R	H	HR	RBI	AVG
23 Years	3,298	12,364	2,174	3,771	755	2,297	.305

Table 1.1. Selected Career Statistics of Henry Aaron

From inspection of Table 1.1, and inspection of other data sets detailing career hitting statistics, it becomes clear that Henry Aaron was unarguably one of the very best hitters in the history of the game. In fact, he has more Runs Batted In (2,297) than anyone in history, and 755 career home runs were the most ever until Barry Bonds broke the record in 2007 with 762 home runs. Unfortunately for Barry Bonds, his record will always be in doubt due to his use of performance-enhancing drugs[1]. Because of the Bonds controversy,

---

[1] Bonds has admitted to performance-enhancing drug use, but he clarifies this by stating he never "knowingly" took performance-enhancing drugs.

Henry Aaron is still considered the "home-run king" by many.

Getting back to my point, this is essentially what I thought statistics was all about – studying a bunch of numbers – something similar to looking over baseball cards to learn about a player's success. I couldn't have been more wrong.

While studying over a bunch of numbers, such as numbers on a baseball card, can be considered a part of statistics, it is a very small part of statistics.

Statistics in its most general form, is learning about the population. Of course, learning about the population requires us to study the population, which is quite difficult, given the size of the population. To alleviate this problem, we collect data about the population, and this sample data is used to help us learn about the population.

While that might sound easy enough, we need to be careful on how we gather the data. It is imperative that our data be randomly sampled so as to avoid any sort of bias.

Here's an example of biased sampling. Suppose you've been given an assignment to estimate the average home price in the US. You happen to live in Brentwood, California. The easy thing to do would be to find the recent real estate transactions in your neighborhood (Brentwood), compute the average transaction price and report it as the average home price in the US.

The problem with this is pretty clear. The sample is not representative of the US population. Brentwood, California is a very affluent area, and the average home price there would be much higher than it would be for the entire US. Instead, we have to *randomly* select homes from all over the US to use for our analysis. When observations are randomly selected for our analysis, any sort of bias is avoided, and we are speaking on behalf of the population. Figure 1.1 shows a generalized version of random sampling, where the "dots" are randomly selected observations within the larger population – the boundaries of the rectangle represent the population boundaries.

Figure 1.1. Sample Data Taken from a Population

Once we have gathered our random sample from the population, we can make a proper analysis. Our intent is to learn something about our data, so that we can "tell the world" about our findings. When we "tell the world" about our findings, we are expected to use a very well-defined set of tools and semantics to articulate our findings. Quite often, we must perform a structured "test" prior to our telling the world about our findings. This formal test essentially demonstrates that proper protocol has been followed in our analyses.

In the scientific research community, any sort of substantial claim is not taken seriously unless appropriate statistical testing accompanies the claim. The business community may not be as rigid as the scientific research community, but carrying out the appropriate analyses and testing is definitely required in most situations.

Consider a company that is about to embark upon a new advertising campaign for their product. Before spending the millions of dollars to launch the campaign, they will need to "field test" the advertising campaign on focus groups, to determine if the focus groups are favorably responsive to the new advertising campaign. In order to make this determination, formal statistical analyses must be performed that convince senior management that the investment in the campaign is worthwhile.

Another example relates to the Federal Food and Drug Administration (FDA) and their possible approval of a new drug. Their job is to make certain a particular drug is effective without any dangerous side-effects. In order approve a new drug, the FDA must have *substantial statistical proof* of the drug's effectiveness without dangerous side-effects.

The formal statistical tools used to assist in such determinations and decisions are briefly described in the next section.

1.1 Tools for this Course

Given this book is for introductory purposes, a "survey" of topics are presented. They are as follows:

• *Descriptive Statistics*, which are the fundamental building block of all subsequent subjects. Here, we describe data sets in the most fundamental form possible, both numerically and graphically.

• *Probability*, which is the study of uncertainty and the likelihood of an event.

• *Random Variables*, which study the structure of certain types of data distributions.

• *Estimation*, which is how we sample from a larger population in our effort to estimate some entity and establish an interval of a specific probabilistic certainty.

• *Hypothesis Testing* is the most important topic we cover. When we make a specific claim about something, it must be accompanied by a formal test. Hypothesis testing provides us with exact structure we must use to support or refute the claim.

• *Simple Linear Regression* is another major topic in this book. In simple linear regression, we explore the possible relationship between two numerical entities. If there is a meaningful relationship, we can exploit this relationship for purposes of estimation and/or prediction of one entity given a specific value of the other entity.

• *Decision Analysis* is where we decide upon alternatives when future uncertainty is inherent. We made decisions using various strategies and we place a valuation on the degree of uncertainty.

1.2 Conclusions

It is reasonable for us to think of statistics as a "toolbox" for us to better understand our environment via a collection of data. These tools help us assess our environment. When we better understand our environment, we can improve and enhance the position of our organization, whatever that particular organization's purpose may be.

1.3 Exercises

1. Would Boston, Massachusetts be a good place to sample in order to estimate the average SAT score for all high school students? Why or why not?

2. Would the state of Ohio be a good place to sample the customer's liking to a new food product? Why or why not?

3. Why might the FDA's use of statistics be more important than other organizations use of statistics?

2. Excel Tutorial

Microsoft is the most commonly used tool for data analysis. First released in 1987, it quickly became the analysis tool of choice. It is by no means a specialized tool. Instead, it is a general-purpose tool that can do many different things, and is known for its flexibility. Not only does Excel have the ability to make a variety of computations, it also has very powerful graphical and data management capabilities.

There is no possible way that this chapter can provide a comprehensive introduction to Excel, but the bare basics are covered, so as to minimize the time needed to become competent.

2.1 Introduction to Excel

Excel is a "spreadsheet" tool, comprised of rows and columns. This format enables the user to organize and analyze data in a tabular format, which simplifies the task. Figure 2.1 shows an example spreadsheet (the terms "spreadsheet" and "worksheet" are used interchangeably).

	A	B	C	D	E	F
1		2019	2018	2017	2016	2015
2	Revenue	$ 2,500,000	$ 2,875,000	$ 3,306,250	$ 3,802,188	$ 4,372,516
3	Expenses	$ 2,000,000	$ 2,280,000	$ 2,599,200	$ 2,963,088	$ 3,377,920
4						
5	Net Profit (Loss)	$ 500,000	$ 595,000	$ 707,050	$ 839,100	$ 994,595
6						
7	Shares Outstanding	9,000,000	9,050,000	9,100,000	9,150,000	9,150,000
8						
9	Profit Per Share	$ 0.0556	$ 0.0657	$ 0.0777	$ 0.0917	$ 0.1087

Figure 2.1. Excel Worksheet Example

At the top of the worksheet, there is a green area, frequently referred to as the "ribbon" or "toolbar." You will see "File | Home | Insert …" toward the top. These items permit the user to configure the worksheet as needed. Below this section, there are several tools that also permit the user to configure the work as needed. In the data section, there are row and column identifiers ("1," "2," "3," etc. for rows; "A," "B," "C," etc. for columns). These row and column identifiers are important, as they provide specific locations for any relevant data. For example, "B2" is the specific location for Revenue for he year 2019, which happens to be $2,500,000.

2.2 Entering and Editing Data

How was the value of $2,500,000 entered in Excel? Very carefully as it turns out. The first thing to do is to "navigate" to cell B2. Navigation can be done via clicking on the arrow keys (←,↑, →, ↓), or by clicking the mouse after hovering over cell B2. From there, the characters "2500000" are typed into cell B2. This value does not look particularly good, so it would be a good idea to format it accordingly. This can be done by clicking on the "$" button toward the top of the worksheet. This will result in the value being displayed as "$2,500,000.00." To eliminate the two decimals, the "Decrease Decimal" button can be clicked twice to display the desired value shown in Figure 2.1. The remaining Revenue, Expenses and Shares Outstanding figures are entered in a similar fashion.

2.3 Calculating with Excel

In the early days of Microsoft Excel, it was mainly used as a computational tool. We could perform basic mathematical functions, copy, paste and so on. Since the late 1980s, however, Excel's capabilities have expanded immensely. Excel now has the ability to perform very complex analyses – fortunately, we will stick to the basic data analyses.

2.3.1   Formulae

For this example, the Profit needs to be calculated. There are several ways to do this. First, we need to navigate to cell B5, the location for Net Profit (Loss) for 2019. To start our calculation, we start our computation with "=" – this informs Excel that a calculation is being entered. In cell B5, we can literally enter "=B2-B3" then hit <Enter>. While this will work, there is a better, more intuitive way. First, we start our calculation in cell B5 and start with the "=". From there we "point" to cell B2 via the arrow keys, then click on the "-" key, then "point" to cell B3 via the arrow keys, and hit <Enter>. This will result in the value we see in cell B5. Additional Formatting may be needed to achieve the "$" symbol and desired rounding.

To calculate Profit Per Share, navigate to cell B9, and enter the following formula: "=B5/B7." Alternatively, navigate to cell B9 and enter "=", followed by pointing to cell B5, then entering "/", then pointing to cell B7 then hit <Enter>. Then format as desired. Either way works.

2.3.2   Copying and Pasting

We could perform the above for the remaining Net Profit (Loss) calculations, but there is an easier way – we can "copy" the recently formatted cell and "paste" it into the appropriate cells. While in cell B5, we enter the following command: <Control-C>. That is, hold down the <Control> key, and then strike the <C> key. This copies the formula for cell B5 into memory. At the bottom of the worksheet, you will see the following message: "Select destination and press ENTER or choose Paste." At this point, the destination range for the copied formula needs to be selected. The desired destination is comprised of cells C5, D5, E5, and F5. The mouse can be used to select this range, by clicking and dragging the mouse from cells C5 through F5. Once this range is selected, hit the <Enter> key and the proper formula will have been copied to these cells.

Another way to select the destination is to, after copying navigate to cell C5, hold down the <Shift> key and navigate to cell F5 (via the "→" key), then hit <Enter>. This approach eliminates the need to use the mouse.

To copy "Profit / Share" to the remaining cells, copy the contents of cell B9 (via <Control><C>) and then paste to cells C9 through F9, either via painting the destination cells, or by holding down <Shift> and the "→" key to cover cells C9 through F9.

A final thought regarding copying and pasting relates to the "Edit" toolbar item. "Copy" and "Paste" can also be done via this approach. However, this approach is time-consuming and the "shortcuts" described above will be preferred, particularly after the students gains experience and confidence with Excel.

2.3.3   Functions

For common mathematical computations, we can use Excel 's built-in functions for assistance. For example, if we wanted to compute the total "Net Profit (Loss)" for the five values in Figure 2.1, we can simply navigate to the cell of choice, use the function "=sum($B5:F5$)." Here, $B5:F5$ is simply the range of the values we wish to average, and this range can be either "painted" by clicking and dragging the mouse, or via using the <Shift> and "→" keys. We can either literally type "=sum($B5:F5$)", or we can type "=average(", then paint our desired range, followed by typing ")" than then hitting<Enter>.

As another example, assume that it is desired to calculate the average "Profit Per Share" for each of the five years in our data set. To do this, we first navigate to our cell of choice and then literally type in the following: "=average($B9:F9$)". Again, "$B9:F9$" is our input range, and it can be selected via the approaches described above.

The "sum" and "average" functions are just two of many functions that are available in Excel. As of this writing, there are 467 functions available. These functions do a variety of things, making data analysis, mathematics, statistics, data management, etc. much easier. The functions relevant to this class would be covered on an as-needed basis.

2.4 Charting with Excel

Excel isn't just for making calculations. When Microsoft Windows became the chosen operating system for IBM-format personal computers in the late 1980s, Excel provided built-in graphical capabilities. This enabled users to create graphical output, enable numerical data to be visualized. It turns out that management types much prefer graphical output as compared to numerical output.

While Excel helps us create many different kinds of charts, we will cover the most basic types here.

2.4.1   Column / Bar Chart

One of the most common types of charts used in commerce is the bar chart (also known as column chart). This type of chart articulates how often certain outcomes occur. The horizontal axis of the chart is a list of possible outcomes – these possible outcomes are often "ordered," or "sorted." The vertical axis is how often each specific outcome occurred, which is often referred to as the frequency. Consider the example below, where we have a sorted listing of the grades in a specific class, and how often each grade occurred.

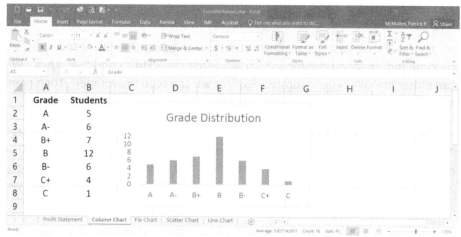

Figure 2.2. Column Chart.

The number of outcomes for each specific grade are listed in the range *B2:B8*. To create a column chart, we paint this particular data range. Then we go to the toolbar on top, and select Insert | Chart | Column Chart. We then select the type of chart we wish to have, whatever that might be. We will have the bars at the proper height, but the horizontal axis will have labels: 1, 2, 3. , which we do not want — we want an actual listing of the appropriate outcomes. To fix this, we click the "Select Data" button. We then click the button to edit the "Horizontal (Category) Axis Labels." We then paint the appropriate list of grades. After some cosmetic formatting and editing, we see a picture similar to that shown in Figure 2.2.

2.4.2   Pie Chart

A pie chart is a chart which details the components of some entity. Continuing with the data set from our last example, we can use a pie chart to detail the relative contributions of each grade outcome. To do this, we once again select the range *B2:B8*. We then select Insert | Chart | Pie Chart. This will produce a primitive version of a pie chart with the legend outcomes of 1, 2, 3, etc. To make the legend more informative, we click the "Select Data" button, and edit the "Horizontal (Category) Axis Labels," and paint the appropriate grade outcomes.

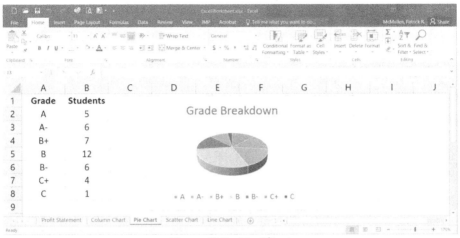

Figure 2.3. Pie Chart

After some cosmetic formatting and editing, the result will be similar to what is shown if Figure 2.3. The color of each "wedge" corresponds with the chart legend. The size of each "wedge" is the relative contribution of each possible outcome. In this example, we see that a grade of "B" was the most common outcome (the yellow wedge), while a grade of "C" was the least common outcome (the purplish wedge).

2.4.3   Scatter Chart

Quite often, a data set has two specific characteristics. For example, we could collect data on daily sales for a small ice cream stand, where one characteristic is the day's high temperature, and the other characteristic is the day's ice cream sales. It would stand to reason that ice cream sales would be higher on warmer days. This sort of data set permits us to explore possible relationships between the characteristics of Temperature and Sales. Excel enables us to explore these possible relationships via it Scatter Chart tool.

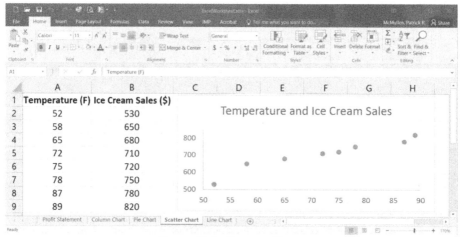

Figure 2.4. Scatter Chart

To plot the data from the figure above, we paint the data range *A2:B9*. The Temperature column represents the horizontal component of the data, whilst the *Ice Cream Sales* column represents the vertical component of the data. After painting the desired data range, we select Insert | Chart |Scatter Chart, and then select the type of chart we desire. After some cosmetic editing, we see the scatter chart above. It should be pointed out that there appears to be a relationship between Temperature and Ice Cream sales – but this will be further explored in the Linear Regression Chapter of the book.

2.4.4 Line Chart

A line chart permits us to visualize a data pattern for intervals evenly spaced apart. These evenly-spaced intervals are usually of a temporal nature. That is, over time. We can use a line plot to visualize how some entity changes over time. To illustrate, let us consider the subscribers Netflix has had since 2011. The relevant data is listed in Figure 2.5.

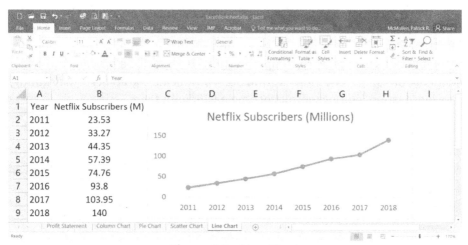

Figure 2.5. Line Chart

We first paint the data in the range B2:B9. From there, we select Insert | Chart | Line Chart, and then select the desired type of line chart. Once this displays, we need to add the appropriate year by clicking the "Select Data" button. From there, we click the edit "Horizontal (Category) Axis Labels," button and paint the appropriate Years. After some minor formatting changes, we should end up with the chart above.

2.5 Worksheet and Workbooks.

If one pays careful attention to the examples developed in Figures 2.1 – 2.5, one might notice that all of these spreadsheets are in a file named "ExcelWorksheet.xls." This file is classified as a "workbook." The workbook has a total of five "worksheets." The leftmost worksheet has the name "Profit Statement," the second has the name "Column Chart," and so on. These worksheet names appear toward the bottom of the spreadsheet. Worksheets can be added via the encircled "+" symbol, and worksheets can be deleted by right-clicking on the worksheet name and hitting the <Delete> key.

It should also be noted that calculations and graphics can be made by using multiple worksheets at the same time. This, however, is beyond the scope of our current interest. It might help to think of a workbook as a collection of worksheets, and each worksheet serves a purpose in the overall project.

25

2.6 Concluding Comments

This is a VERY brief tutorial on becoming acquainted with Microsoft Excel. This tutorial is only intended to familiarize you with the most basic of Excel's functionality. The best way to gain competence in Excel is by experience. Excel functions necessary to compute various things will be provided on an as-needed basis. Entering formulae, producing graphics, navigating, copying/pasting, editing will all become easier with time.

3. Describing Data

Statistics is all about studying data and articulating to the world our findings. Prior to our performing formal statistical tests, we need to describe the data in its most basic form. There are three basic approaches to doing this: Categorical Data Analysis, Numerical Data Analysis and the Presenting of Graphical Data.

3.1 Categorical Data Analysis

Describing categorical data is mainly a "low-tech," common sense exercise. Data of a "categorical" nature means that the data is not in numerical form, but in the form of categories. These categories are sometimes referred to as "buckets" or "bins." There is not much we can do with this data other than organizing it into a table and/or a simple chart.

For example, let's assume an apparel company is interested in targeting a demographic that frequently attends rock concerts. They are most interested in getting a handle on the color of trousers the patrons wear. As such, they hire people at the concert to tally the number of people who wear certain color jeans. They have decided on four categories: "black," "blue," "beige" and "other." In addition to the color category, they also categorize patrons by gender. After the tally, they simply present their findings in a table where each category combination is totaled, and the Gender rows are summed. The results might appear as shown in Table 3.1a.

	Black	Blue	Beige	Other	Total
Male	236	326	73	22	657
Female	158	75	42	31	306

Table 3.1a. Tally of Jeans by Gender

We can take this analysis one-step further if we present a percent breakdown of the jeans' color by gender. To do this for the men, we would divide 236 by 657 to get the percentage of black jeans, divide 326 by 657 to get the percentage of blue jeans, and so on. When we do the same for the women (dividing the frequency of each color by 306), we have the results shown in Table 3.1b.

	Black	Blue	Beige	Other	Total
Male	35.92%	49.62%	11.11%	3.35%	100%
Female	51.63%	24.51%	13.73%	10.13%	100%

Table 3.1b. Percentage of Jeans Color by Gender

Table 3.1b is probably a better way to express this data, as percentages put the tallies in a more standardized perspective as compared to raw counts.

Another way to express this data is to organize it into a column chart, where the height of each column is the percentage of jeans color, and this is done for both male and females. This particular chart was created via the "Column Chart" feature in Microsoft Excel. A pie chart is another option to show this data, where the size of each slice/wedge is the percentage of a specific color, but in recent years, the statistics community has discouraged used of pie charts because it is believed that pie charts distort perspective. As such, the column chart is shown as the preferred graphical tool for tallied data.

Figure 3.1. Column Chart of Jeans Color by Gender

3.2 Numerical Data Analysis

This is where our opportunity to analyze data really begins. With descriptive statistics, we can take a given set of data, calculate many statistics, and then articulate our findings in a reasonable way. There are several categories in which to describe data, but we concentrate on the most important two categories: expectation and variation.

3.2.1   Expectation

Expectation is a measure of central tendency – a singular value we can use to describe the expectation of a given data set. For example, when an instructor administers an exam, they will often state the exam average for the entire class. The instructor has summed the test scores, and divided this sum by the number of exams taken. The instructor is articulating, in essence, how the average student performed on the exam. Based upon a specific student's score then, any given student can compare their performance against the average performance. In the world of statistics, the average value of some entity is often called the **mean**.

Mathematically, we define the sample mean ($\bar{x}$) as follows, where x_i is a specific observation, referred to as the ith observation, and n refers to the number of observations in our sample. Our sample mean is as follows:

$$\bar{x} = \frac{1}{n}\sum_{i=1}^{n} x_i \qquad \text{(Eq. 3-1)}$$

The average isn't the only metric we can use to articulate central tendency. Consider a situation in which we are given an assignment to estimate the expected home value in King County, Washington. We decide to randomly sample 10 houses in the area for our estimation. It turns out that one of the ten houses we use is the home of Microsoft founder Bill Gates. Mr. Gates' home is worth several million dollars – much higher than the other home values in our collection of data. This will severely bias our average – it would inflate our average and misrepresent the expected home value in King County, Washington. Instead of calculating the average, we can sort our data from low to high (or high to low) and selected the "middle value" for an odd number of observations, or average the "middle two" values for an even number of observations. This value is called the **median**, and is often used on socioeconomic data to eliminate any biases associated with extreme values.

Another measure of central tendency, although perhaps not as important as the mean and standard deviation is the **mode** – the most frequently observed value in a collection of data. Sometimes, depending on the nature of the data, there will not be a mode. Sometimes, there may be multiple modes. For example, where a data set contains two unique modes, the data can be referred to as "bi-model."

In Microsoft Excel, the built-in functions for the measures of central tendency are shown in Table 3.2. In this context, and throughout the book, the term *"data range"* refers to the actual data set being referred to while in Excel.

Statistic	Excel Formula
Mean	=average(*data range*)
Median	=median(*data range*)
Model	=mode(*data range*)

Table 3.2. Excel Formulae for Central Tendency

3.2.2 Variation

Variation is an underappreciated and overlooked part of descriptive statistics, but a very important one. In fact, it is just as important as the measures of central tendency. The reason it is so underappreciated is because it is not terribly well understood. In fact, when I didn't do well the first time I took statistics, my misunderstanding of variation was a large reason why.

Variation measures dispersion of the data set. That is the most general form of variation, which we can capture that value by the **range** (*Range*), which is the difference between the minimum observed value (x_{min}) and the maximum observed value (x_{max}). Mathematically, this is as follows:

$$Range = x_{max} - x_{min} \qquad \text{(Eq. 3-2)}$$

While this version of dispersion is simple to calculate, it is naïve because it does not account for dispersion of the observations with respect to the mean. The value that best captures dispersion about the mean is the **sample standard deviation**, s. At first glance, the mathematics of this equation may seem intimidating, but with some explanation, it should become more understandable. The sample standard deviation is as following:

$$s = \sqrt{\frac{\sum_{i=1}^{n}(x_i - \bar{x})^2}{n-1}} \qquad \text{(Eq. 3-3)}$$

This calculation calculates the difference between each observation and the sample mean. This difference is squared. It is squared for two reasons: the first reason is to eliminate a negative number in the calculation, as any number squared is a positive number; the second reason is to amplify big differences between the observed value and the sample mean. These squared differences are then summed, which accounts for the numerator of the equation. The numerator is then divided by (n - 1). The division by n is to put the calculated quantity into the same units as the observed data – similar to dividing by n when a sample mean is calculated. The value of "1" is subtracted from n to account for the fact that we have limited data – sample information instead of population data. The subtraction of "1" from n adjusts the sample standard deviation upward, "inflating" our estimate of the standard deviation, as compared to the standard deviation of the population. Fortunately, this formula is rarely used in practice, as Excel and other software packages easily make the calculation.

Another formula, used to calculate the sample variance is the squared value of the sample standard deviation, and is shown here:

$$s^2 = \frac{\sum_{i=1}^{n}(x_i - \bar{x})^2}{n - 1} \qquad \text{(Eq. 3-4)}$$

The only difference between the two is that the sample standard deviation is the square root of the sample variance, and is more commonly used, because its value is in the same units as the observed value.

In Excel, the formulae for range, standard deviation and sample variance are as follows:

Statistic	Excel Formula
Range	=max(*data range*) – min(*data range*)
Sample Standard Deviation	=stdev(*data range*)
Sample Variance	=var(*data range*)

Table 3.3. Excel Formulae for Variation

Now that we have the tools to describe central tendency and variation, a brief time is spent discussing the distribution of the data set.

3.2.3 Distribution

Many observations comprise a data set. Each individual observation has a "position" in the data set, so to speak. When the data is sorted, we can "see" where a certain observation fits in with the rest of the data. Excel, JMP and other software packages tell provide us with the position of an observation in a data set without our having to sort or otherwise manipulate the data. In particular, we can calculate **percentiles** and **quantiles** associated with a data set.

The percentile of an observation in a data set is its relative position to other observations in that same data set. You should be familiar with this concept. If/when you took the GMAT, SAT or ACT exam, you were given a numerical score which probably didn't mean much to you, because you have no basis for comparison. But you were also presented with percentile data, which told you how you did when compared to the performance of *all* test-takers. For example, if your percentile score was 75, you scored better than 75% of all test-takers.

The percentile of a data set basically breaks down the data into 100 pieces, or percentiles. The quartile of a data set basically breaks down the data into four pieces. The first quartile is tantamount to the 25th percentile, the second quartile is tantamount to the 50th percentile (which we also refer to as the median), and the third quartile is tantamount to the 75th percentile. The fourth quartile, which we never use, is essentially the maximum observed value.

In Excel, these values are easily computed using the *percentile* and *quartile* functions.

Statistic	Excel Formula
Percentile	=percentile(*data range, value*)
Quartile	=quartile(*data range, quartile value*)

Table 3.4. Excel Formulae for Percentiles and Quartiles

For example, if we have a data set called "X" with several observations, the function "=percentile(X, 0.63)" will return the value in the data set associated with the 63rd percentile. If we use the function "=quartile(X, 3)," the function will return the value in the data set associated with the 3rd quartile (or 75th percentile). Note that for the percentile function, our value must be between 0 and 1. The 0th percentile is the minimum value in the data set, while the 100th percentile is the maximum value in the data set. For quartile values, our quartile value must be either 0, 1, 2, 3 or 4. The 0th quartile is the minimum value in the data set, while the 4th quartile is the maximum value in the data set. It should be noted, however, that the 0th quartile and the 4th quartile are of no practical value, as they respectively imply the minimum and maximum values.

It should be noted that the functions shown in Table 3.4 assume that we intend for the highest value possible to occur – as in a test score, for example. If we seek the lowest score possible, we simply replace "=percentile(*data range*, *value*)" with "1 – percentile(*data range*, *value*)." For quartiles, we simply switch the values for the first and third quartiles.

We have restricted our coverage of "distribution" to percentiles and quartiles. There are other measures of distribution, such as **skewness** and **kurtosis** which are beyond the scope of this book. In the next section, we will continue to discuss the distribution of a data set, but in a more conceptual manner.

3.3 Presenting Graphical Data

A picture is worth a thousand words. Statistics is no exception to that adage. Today's computer and software resources have greatly enhanced our ability to visualize data. Thirty years ago, our ability to visualize data was essentially constrained to a handheld calculator, pencil and paper. Bad memories. ☹

While there are countless tools to present data in a graphical format, our pursuit of presenting graphical data will be confined to the **histogram** and the **boxplot**.

3.3.1   Histogram

Without question, the histogram is the most common way to graphically present **univariate** (single variable) data. When we have a collection of data, it is wise to organize the data based on similarity – we did this in Section 2.1, where we categorized the jeans that the concert-goers wore by gender and by the color of jeans. Now that we are dealing with numerical data, similarity can be categorized much easier. Numbers that are "similar" can be numbers that are close in value. In a histogram, we have two axes: the horizontal axis (often referred to as the "x-axis") is a listing of numerical outcomes in ascending order. The vertical axis (often referred to as the "y-axis") is the **frequency** (how often) each outcome was observed. A histogram is sometimes referred to a frequency chart.

Outcome is a subjective assessment and some thought is required as to how to manage outcomes. For example, if I were give an exam to my students, the minimum score might be 70 while the maximum score might be 100. The outcomes would be easy to itemize: 70, 71, 72, ..., 100. This, however, is only one way to structure outcomes. As critic of this approach might think there is too much detail in these outcomes, particularly if the class is small. They might suggest fewer outcomes, perhaps only even-numbered scores: 70, 72, 74, ..., 100. Under this revised scenario, odd-numbered scores would be placed into the lower category or higher category – it really doesn't matter, provided all odd-numbered scores are treated the same.

The point of the above is to suggest that some thought should go into how outcomes are organized. One rule of thumb is that a good number of categories to use when deciding how many outcomes to have is a function of the number of observations in the data set, which we will call "n." This particular rule of thumb suggests that $\sqrt{n}$ is a good number of categories to use. I agree with this rule of thumb, but I generalize it even more – for large data sets (~ 500 observations), I like to use about 25 categories. For larger data sets (≥ 1000 observations), I like to use about 30 or so categories. Fortunately, most fully-dedicated statistical software packages like JMP and R automatically choose how many categories to use, but this can be controlled by the user. For Excel, the number of categories must be pre-determined.

Let's build a histogram with some data. Let's assume that it was "Las Vegas Night" at the business school. Staff, students and faculty played a few casino games for small amounts of money, and the "money lost" by the players went to a charitable cause. There were 120 participants, and their "winnings" are shown below in Table 3.5. Negative winnings are, of course, losses and are preceded by a "minus sign."

From close inspection of Table 3.5, the worst performance was a loss of $10.00, and the best performance was a gain of $2.00, making for a range of -10 to 2. It seems reasonable to have categories starting at -$10 and ending with $2, and having them in $1 increments, for a total of 13 categories. Incidentally, 13 total categories is reasonably close to the rule of thumb number of categories of $\sqrt{n}$.

-3.75	-6.00	-8.50	-2.75	-0.50	-5.50	-6.00	-4.75	-6.50	-5.25
-7.50	-6.75	-4.75	-3.25	-5.75	-1.00	-1.00	-5.50	-5.75	-3.75
-1.75	0.75	-0.75	-0.50	-2.00	1.75	-2.75	1.75	-5.75	-2.50
-2.25	-1.25	-3.25	-5.75	-5.25	-3.00	-6.25	-5.25	-4.75	-7.75
-3.25	-2.25	-2.00	-4.50	-3.00	-8.25	-4.00	0.00	0.75	-1.50
-6.75	-2.25	-4.25	-6.25	-7.25	-2.50	1.25	-1.75	-3.00	-4.75
-9.50	-4.50	-4.25	-1.50	-4.25	-8.50	-3.00	-2.25	-3.00	-5.50
-5.00	-3.75	-4.25	-2.25	-3.75	-1.25	-6.50	-5.50	-6.50	-5.25
-0.75	-3.00	-4.50	-1.75	-3.00	-4.50	-2.50	-2.25	-4.50	-6.00
-3.50	-6.00	-2.25	-6.00	-3.50	-6.00	-0.75	-2.75	-1.50	-1.50
-3.25	-8.50	-2.75	-4.75	-6.25	-1.00	0.25	-5.00	-3.50	-10.00
-7.25	-2.75	-1.75	-2.00	-2.25	-3.25	2.00	-3.50	-0.50	-8.25

Table 3.5. Winnings from Las Vegas Night

The histogram can be generated in Excel via Data | Data Analysis | Histogram. From there, you are asked for two groups of data: the first is the "Input Data," which is the 120 actual observations; the second is the "Bin Range," which is an ordered list of categories, which, in this case, is -$10, -$9, ..., $1, $2. Excel then returns the frequencies of each categorized outcome, which is shown in Table 3.6.

Outcome Category	Frequency	Relative Frequency
-$10	1	0.83%
-$9	1	0.83%
-$8	5	4.17%
-$7	4	3.33%
-$6	14	11.67%
-$5	14	11.67%
-$4	15	12.50%
-$3	20	16.67%
-$2	19	15.83%
-$1	13	10.83%
$0	7	5.83%
$1	3	2.50%
$2	4	3.33%

Table 3.6. Frequencies of "Winnings" from Las Vegas Night

A histogram using the frequency data from Table 2.6 is shown in Figure 3.2.

Figure 3.2. Histogram of Las Vegas Night

You will notice from Figure 3.2 that this histogram is nothing more than a column chart, with the horizontal axis being the ordered categories, and the vertical axis being the frequencies.

It should also be noticed that the rightmost column of Table 2.6 is entitled **"Relative Frequency."** For each outcome category, we can convert the frequencies to relative frequencies by dividing the frequency value by the total number of observations, which is 120 in this case. For example, the -$4 category has a frequency of 15. The relative frequency of this category is 12.50% (15/120). It would be of no particular benefit to show a histogram of the relative frequencies, because the column heights would be exactly proportion to the column heights of the frequency histogram in Figure 3.2. The only difference between a frequency and a relative frequency is that the frequencies will sum to the number of observations, while the sum of the relative frequencies will sum to 1.

In terms of the histogram itself, we see that losses of about $3 is the most frequent outcome. Without getting into descriptive statistics at present, we can reasonably conclude some form of central tendency of an approximate $3 loss. This will be discussed further in the next section.

Figure 3.3 shows a very nice example of a histogram. It illustrates income distribution in 2011. The horizontal axis shows annual income categories in $5,000, where the vertical axis shows the relative frequencies of these outcomes.

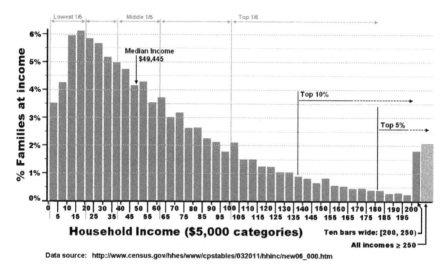

Figure 3.3. Histogram of Income Distribution

The histogram has a few properties worth noting. First, we might notice that most outcomes reside on the left – lower incomes, with a decreasing frequency of higher incomes, until we get to the $200K and more category. The median, a measure of central tendency, resides in the "hump," while there is a dominant tail to the right. We use the term "**skewed right**" to describe this type of distribution – the tail is to the right of the "hump." A distribution that is "**skewed left**" is where the dominant tail is to the left of the "hump." If a distribution is not skewed either way, we call the distribution **symmetric**.

3.3.2   Box Plot

As stated earlier, the histogram is the most important tool we have to present descriptive statistical data in graphical form. The **box plot**, however, does provide us with additional insight regarding the distribution. The box plot is more of an abstraction than the histogram and requires some explanation. The box plot shows us the first quartile, the second quartile (median) and the third quartile as vertical lines composing a box. The first quartile is the left edge of the box, while the third quartile is the right edge of the box. The median is somewhere between these two edges. We then compute "thresholds" or "fences" to determine "**outliers**." There is a lower threshold and an upper threshold. Each of these are 1.5 times the interquartile range ($Q_3 - Q_1$). Mathematically, these thresholds are determined as follows:

$$\text{Lower Threshold} = Q_1 - 1.5*(Q_3 - Q_1) \qquad \text{(Eq. 3-5)}$$

$$\text{Upper Threshold} = Q_3 + 1.5*(Q_3 - Q_1) \qquad \text{(Eq. 3-6)}$$

Any values that are below the lower threshold or above the upper threshold are considered outliers – extreme observations. "Whiskers" are then drawn in. The lower whisker is drawn from the first quartile to correspond to the smallest value In the data set above the lower threshold. Similarly, the upper whisker is drawn from the third quartile to the highest value in the data set below the upper threshold. Values in the data set outside of these two thresholds are considered outliers and are highlighted as such. It is possible for a box plot *not* to have outliers. The figure below shows a generalized box plot in the context as described.

It is important to note that various books and software packages give slightly different treatments to boxplots, particularly with respect to how whiskers and outliers are determined. What is consistent, however, for all box plots, is that the first and third quartiles, along with the median are always given the same treatment.

3.4 Putting it All Together

This section is concerned with making a proper statistical reporting given a data set, and using our descriptive statistical tools and our graphical tools. For illustrative purposes, we will use our Las Vegas Night data set, and JMP to assist with the analysis.

Once the JMP software is started, we can import an Excel data set. From there, asking JMP to make the statistical analyses is very easy. While in JMP, we select "Analyze," then "Distribution." From there, we select our variable for the "Y, Columns" box and click "Go." At this point, JMP returns an immense amount of output, most of which we do not need. Once we are in output mode, we can eliminate which output we do not wish to see, and focus on what we do want to see, by unchecking various output options – this (selecting which output to see) is something that requires experimentation. The figure below is a JMP screen capture of our Las Vegas Night analyses – all of these outputs are standard with JMP.

Figure 3.4. JMP Output of Las Vegas Night Data

The first thing I notice is that the average winnings are -$3.73. In other words, I can expect to lose $3.73, which is quite similar to the median value of -$3.5. I also notice a standard deviation of $2.49, and first and third quartiles of -$5.5 and -$2.06. The next thing I do is examine the histogram, which is essentially the same as Figure 3.2. Here, the x-axis of the histogram was manipulated to see increments of $1.

A very nice feature of JMP is that it places a box plot on top of the histogram – this permits us to the see the relationship between the two graphical tools, providing us a better perspective of the data set. JMP offers two box plot features not shown via other software packages. In the box plot, you will notice a diamond-shaped figure. The part of the diamond where it is at its maximum height is the mean value of the data set. The width of the diamond shows us a 95% confidence interval, which we will talk about in Chapter 6. The red bracket just above the box plot is referred to as the "shortest half," which displays the highest-density collection of 50% of the observations in the data set.

Earlier in my teaching career, I never covered the box plot. I restricted my conversation to the histogram when covering graphical approaches to descriptive statistics. In recent years, however, I have come to embrace the box plot. While it is definitely less concrete than the histogram, it does provide us with a tremendous amount of information in a particularly simple way. As such, I now consider it an enhancement to the histogram.

3.5 Conclusions

None of the concepts in this chapter are particularly difficult – I state this from both a mathematical *and* conceptual perspective. Despite the relative simplicity of this subject matter, none of it should be discounted as unimportant. Descriptive statistics is perhaps the most important subject covered in this book. When we talk about a data set, we should ALWAYS summarize the data in numerical/statistical form, and use graphical support, as many people in business, particularly those without a numerical background, place more value on the pictures than they do the numbers.

3.6 Exercises

For problems 1 – 6, use the "ExamScoresData" data set. For problems 7 – 12, use the "WireGaugeData" data set.

The "ExamScoresData" data set records scores for two exams taken by a group of students. The students took Exam 1 prior to their taking Exam 2.

1. Using Excel, please address the following:
   a. The mean values for Exam 1 and Exam 2.
   b. The median values for Exam 1 and Exam 2.
   c. The standard deviation values for Exam 1 and Exam 2.
   d. The lowest score of the two exams, and the highest score of the two exams.
2. Using Microsoft Excel, create a combined histogram for each exam using a bin range in increments of 2 exam points.
3. Using Microsoft Excel, created a combined histogram for each exam using a bin range in increments of 1 exam point.

4. Using your histogram from Problem 3, distinguish the performance between Exam 1 and Exam 2.
5. Do the histograms provide any help in determining how the data is distributed. Comment on the data distributions.
6. Using JMP, construct box plots for Exams 1 and 2. Do your findings support your answer in Problem 4?

For the "WireGaugeData" data set, data was taken from two shifts in a factory where the diameter of 22-gauge wire was measured. It is intended for the wire to have a diameter of 0.64mm.

Using Excel, please compute the following:

7. The mean wire diameter for Shifts 1 and 2.
8. The median wire diameter for Shifts 1 and 2.
9. The standard deviation of the wire diameter for Shifts 1 and 2.
10. Between the two shifts, what is the smallest wire diameter, and what is the largest wire diameter?
11. Using Excel, create a combined histogram using 30 bins, positioned between the minimum and maximum wire diameters.
12. Using JMP, create a box plot for each shift.

13. Using your findings from Problems 7 and 9, talk about the distribution for each shift.
14. Which shift does a better job in achieving the targeted diameter of 0.64mm?
15. Which shift is more consistent in terms of wire diameter?

4. Probability

We encounter probability every day in our lives. We watch the news on TV and learn that there will be a slight chance of rain tomorrow afternoon. Sometimes, a probability of rain will even be given explicitly. If we watch news about politics, we will even see political pundits estimating probabilities of candidates being elected to various forms of political office.

In the specific sense, probability is the likelihood of some event occurring. In the general sense, probability is the study of uncertainty. While this chapter might focus on studying the likelihood of some event occurring, the remainder of the book is certainly more focused on studying uncertainty, as this concept is very important when we turn to hypothesis testing in the latter chapters of this book.

4.1 Basic Probability

This section addresses the most common-sense aspects of probability. Let us begin by referring to some event as "A." The probability of event A occurring is the ratio of how many times A can occur to all trials in the experiment. A simple example is where we are interested in determining the probability of drawing a "6" from a standard deck of 52 cards. We know that there are four different possibilities of "6" in a standard deck of cards (clubs, diamonds, hearts, and spades). There are, then, four cards of "6" in a deck of cards, making our probability of drawing a "6" four chances in 52, or 4/52, which is 7.69%.

The probability of drawing a "6 of clubs" is different than the above probability. The deck of cards has only one card that fits this description. Because of this, our chances of drawing a "6 of clubs" from a standard deck of cards is 1/52, which is 1.92%.

The probability rules in the next section provide some tools that assist us in understanding slightly more complex probabilistic issues.

4.2 Probability Rules

Prior to presenting the actual rules, there are a few terms which need to be defined, so that the probability rules are more clearly understood.

As stated previously, *P(A)* is the notation we use to describe the probability of event A occurring. Related to that is the notation P(A̅), which we refer to as the probability of event A not occurring, or "the probability of **'A-compliment.'"**

Another item of business which must be covered involves **mutually exclusive events** and **independent events**. Mutually exclusive events are events that cannot happen at the same time – events where only one specific outcome can occur. An example of a mutually exclusive event is where we sample from a larger population to study something. Our subjects can only be male or female – never both. As such, the gender of an individual can be thought of as a mutually exclusive event. Another example is a student's application to a university. There are three possible outcomes: acceptance, rejection, or "wait-list." When a student receives their decision letter from a university, the outcome will only be ONE of three possible outcomes, never any combination of the possible outcomes.

Independent events *can* happen at the same time – these events are independent of other events. Let's assume that the New York Yankees are playing the Boston Red Sox tonight. Meanwhile, the Pittsburgh Pirates are playing the Cincinnati Reds. It is possible that both the Yankees and the Pirates win because they are not playing each other – they have other opponents. The Yankees / Red Sox game and the Pirates / Reds games are independent of each other.

To understand the probability rules shown below, it is of great importance to understand the difference between mutually exclusive events and independent events.

4.2.1   Probability Rule 1
The probability of some event will always be between zero and one. A probability can never be less than zero, nor can it be greater than one. Mathematically, this is as follows:

$$0 \leq P(A) \leq 1 \qquad \text{(Eq. 4-1)}$$

This rule applies to both mutually exclusive and independent events.

4.2.2   Probability Rule 2
For mutually exclusive events, only one of the possible events can occur.

If there are four possible events (A, B, C and D), one of them must occur. Mathematically, we can state this as follows:

$$P(A) + P(B) + P(C) + P(D) = 1 \qquad \text{(Eq. 4-2)}$$

4.2.3   Probability Rule 3

If event A does not occur, its complement (A̅) must occur. Mathematically, this means two things:

$$P(A) + P(\bar{A}) = 1 \qquad \text{(Eq. 4-3)}$$

$$P(\bar{A}) = 1 - P(A) \qquad \text{(Eq. 4-4)}$$

This rule applies to both mutually exclusive and independent events.

4.2.4   Probability Rule 4

For mutually exclusive events, the probability of event A or event B occurring is the sum of the probabilities. Mathematically, this can be said as follows:

$$P(A \text{ or } B) = P(A) + P(B) \qquad \text{(Eq. 4-5)}$$

It should also be stated that another way of stating P(A or B) is to say P(A∪B), which implies the "**union**" of A and B. As an example, there is 10% probability that I will have pizza for dinner tonight, and a 15% probability that I will have pasta for dinner. Therefore, there is a 25% probability (10% + 15%) probability that I will have either pizza or pasta for dinner tonight.

4.2.5   Probability Rule 5

For independent events, we can calculate the probability of both events A and B happening via the following relationship:

$$P(A \text{ and } B) = P(A) * P(B) \qquad \text{(Eq. 4-6)}$$

We can also state P(A and B) as P(A ∩ B), which we call the "intersection" of events A and B.

There is a probabilistic tool known as a "**Venn Diagram**," which can help us visualize these types of things. For the independent events A and B, the Venn Diagram provides visual support for the above equation. For example, let us assume that there is a 60% chance the Yankees will beat the Red Sox, and there is a 55% chance that the Pirates will beat the Reds. The probability of both the Yankees and Pirates winning is, therefore, (0.60)(0.55) = 0.33, or 33%. For this calculation, we are essentially calculating the section of the circles that overlap in Figure 4.1.

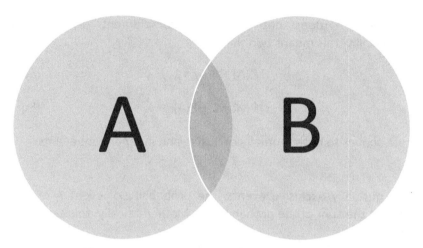

Figure 4.1. Venn Diagram of Events A and B

4.2.6 Probability Rule 6

For independent events, the probability of either events A or B occurring is as follows:

$$P(A \text{ or } B) = P(A) + P(B) - (P(A) * P(B)) \qquad \text{(Eq. 4-7)}$$

Again, the notation P(A or B) can also be shown as $P(A \cup B)$. To continue with our example, the probability of either the Yankees or Pirates winning their game is (0.60 + 0.55 − (0.60 * 0.55)), which is 0.82, or 82%.

4.3 Contingency Tables

There are times when we have the opportunity to study mutually exclusive events where there are two factors involved, as opposed to a single factor as described above. If we have one factor with a possible mutually exclusive outcomes and another factor with b possible mutually exclusive outcomes, we have a **contingency table** with a rows and b columns, and $a*b$

table entries. For each cell in the table, we are given the number of outcomes that are associated with each unique combination of the two factors. This contingency table provides with probabilistic information regarding each factor and all combinations of factor levels.

Consider an example of the US House of Representatives voting on a house resolution – voting on whether or not a bill should become a law. Two factors of interest here are first, the party affiliation – this factor has two levels: Republican and Democrat. The second factor is how the representative voted on the resolution. This factor also has two levels: Yes and No. Because each factor has two levels, we have four combinations. For our example, we study House Resolution 1599, which was brought to the House of Representatives on July 23, 2015. The name of the resolution is the "Safe and Accurate Food Labeling Act." The contingency table of this vote is as follows:

	Yes	No	Total
Republican	230	12	242
Democrat	45	138	183
Total	275	150	425

Table 4.1. House Vote on HR 1599

The first order of business is to determine whether or not the bill passed the house. It did, by a 275 – 150 margin. I look at the column total for "Yes" and I compare it to the column total for "No" to make this determination. I also notice that 242 Republicans voted, while 183 Democrats voted. I make this determination by looking at the row totals. Finally, I arrive at a value of 425 total votes – this value can be determined by adding the row totals *or* the column totals. This value can also be determined by adding the values of the four factor-level combinations (230 + 12 + 45 + 138). 425 is the total number of observations, which we can refer to as *n*.

If we were to divide all numbers in our contingency table by *n*, we would get probabilities, which standardize our frequency data. By doing this, we are essentially building a table of relative frequencies. Table 4.2 shows the results of this.

	Yes	No	Total
Republican	54.12%	2.82%	56.94%
Democrat	10.59%	32.47%	43.06%
Total	64.71%	35.29%	100%

Table 4.2. Relative Frequencies of HR 1599

From Table 4.2, we see that 56.94% of the votes were cast by Republicans, and 43.06% of the votes were cast by Democrats. We also see that 64.71% of the vote was "Yes," while 35.29% of the vote was "No." The political party votes will sum to 100%, while the "Yes" vs "No" votes will also sum to 100%. These values are referred to as "**marginal probabilities**" because they are on the "margins," or edges of the contingency table. In essence, they tell us how each of our factors are divided. We can state these marginal probabilities in mathematical notation as well. For example, we can say the following about Democrats: P(Democrat) = 43.06%.

Figure 4.2 also provides with "**joint probabilities**," values showing us the probability of specific combinations of our factors occurring. For example, 2.82% of Republicans voted No on HR 1599. Note that both factors are considered for this joint probability. We can state this mathematically via the following: P(Repubican and No) = 0.0282. The notation P(Repubican $\cap$ No) is also reasonable notation.

The final topic we discuss relative to contingency tables is the concept of **conditional probability**. The conditional probability of an event occurring is the probability of that event occurring given that some other event has occurred. Mathematically, this is as follows:

$$P(A \mid B) = P(A \cap B) / P(B) \qquad \text{(Eq. 4-8)}$$

In this particular notation, the "|" means "given," so we are implying the probability of A given B. Said as simply as possible, we'd like to find the probability of even A occurring knowing that event B has already occurred.

For example, we can calculate the probability of a voter voting "No" with the prior knowledge that they are a democrat. In the context of this example, we determine this as follows:

$$P(No \mid Democrat) = P(No \cap Democrat) / P(Democrat) \qquad \text{(Eq. 4-9)}$$

The calculation for this would be 0.3247 / 0.4306 = 0.7541. In other words, there is a 75.41% chance that a representative will vote "No" provided they are a Democrat.

If someone votes "Yes," what is the probability they are a Republican? We can address this question as follows:

$$P(Republican \mid Yes) = P(Yes \cap Republican) / P(Yes) \quad \text{(Eq. 4-10)}$$

For this question, we employ 0.5412 / 0.6471, which results in 0.8364. In other words, given that a representative votes "Yes," the probability of them being Republican is 83.64%.

Contingency Tables are a valuable exercise in better understanding probability. We often find useful information in studying outcomes when two variables of the mutually exclusive variety are present. We conclude this chapter by focusing on the number of possible outcomes via a brief introduction to "counting."

4.4 Probability Trees and Multiple Trials

Often there are times when a certain probabilistic entity is repeated several times. Flipping a coin multiple times, playing a series of chess games with an opponent, etc. We can use a tool known as a **probability tree** to analyze the array of outcomes. When random events are repeated over and over, they essentially become independent events. This should make sense given that outcome of a second coin flip is not related to the outcome of the first coin flip.

Each node of a probability tree represents a trial, while each branch of a probability tree represents an outcome. When there are several outcomes, the graphical representation resembles a tree-like structure. As an example, consider the flipping of a "fair" coin three times. Here, a "fair" coin means that the probability of head and tails are the same – both 50%. Figure 3.2 show a probability tree for three trials of a coin toss.

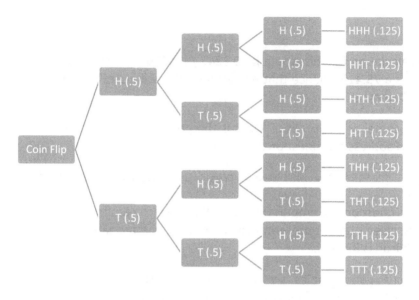

Figure 4.2. Probability Tree for Three Coin Tosses

Notice from Figure 4.2 that there is branching three times – one for each trial, resulting in eight branches. The highlighted nodes furthest to the right summarize each of the eight outcomes, in terms of heads or tails and the associated probability of each outcome. The number of branches in a probability tree can be determined via the following:

$$\text{Branches} = \text{Outcomes}^{\text{Trials}} \qquad \text{(Eq. 4-11)}$$

In our simple example, we have two possible outcomes and three trials, resulting in eight total branches.

We can take the summary nodes, and compile the number of successes (we can use "heads" in our example), and explain them via a histogram so that we can visualize the result of multiple trials. A histogram for our example is shown in Figure 4.3.

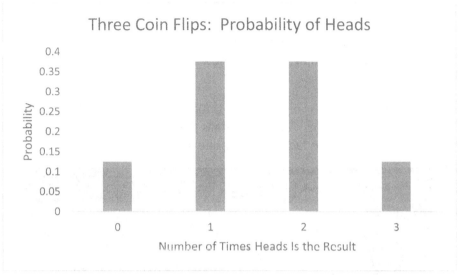

Figure 4.3. Histogram of Three Coin Flips

As a sidenote, we are essentially enumerating here, which can be cumbersome when multiple trials are involved. Fortunately, the binomial distribution can assist us with this issue, which is described in the next chapter.

4.5 Basic Counting

As defined at the beginning of this chapter, the probability of a specific event occurring is the number of possible successes divided by the number of possible outcomes. Quite often, determining the number of possible outcomes is a bit tricky, and quite often, this number is shockingly large. With a few basic mindsets, we can discipline ourselves to finding the number of outcomes by understanding what tools need to be used to make the appropriate calculation. There are three basic approaches we will take: the product rule, understanding combinations, and understanding permutations. This topic is a branch of probability often referred to as **combinatorics**, which is, in my opinion covered too infrequently in our statistics books.

4.5.1 The Product Rule

Often we have a number of factors, each having a specific number of levels. To determine the number of possible outcomes, we can employ the product rule. In its simplest form and from a mathematical perspective, the product rules is as follows

$$\text{Outcomes} = \prod_{i=1}^{m} n_i, \qquad \text{(Eq. 4-12)}$$

Where n_i is the number of levels for factor level i, and the upper case "pi" symbol (Π) means multiply, similar to how the upper "sigma" sign (Σ) means to sum.

As an example, let's consider pizza options. There are four factors: crust, cheese, topping and size. Table 4.3 details these factors. For this example, it is assumed that for each factor, exactly one level is permitted.

Factor	Number of Levels	Levels
Crust	4	Thin, Thick, Deep Dish, Pan
Cheese	4	Mozzarella, Provalone, Romano, Gouda
Topping	30	Anchovy, Bell Pepper, …, Pinapple
Size	4	Individual, Medium, Large, Family

Table 4.3. Pizza Options

The number of unique pizza combinations is simply determined by the product of the number of levels for all factors: (4)*(4)*(30)*(4) = 1,920. This example shows that there are 1,920 outcomes. Of course, some of these outcomes are more likely than others in reality, but that fact is beyond the scope of our present conversation.

4.5.2 Combinations

In the previous paragraph, the word "combination" is used somewhat informally. In this section, we use the word "combination" more formally. Given we have n unique items in a set, and we wish to select a subset of size r from the set, the number of unique combinations we have is often referred to as "n choose r." Another way to state this is C(n, r) or $_nC_r$. For the remainder of this book, the C(n, r) notation will be used. With these definitions now known, the number of combinations can be determined as follows:

$$\text{Combinations} = C(n, r) = \frac{n!}{r!(n-r)!} \qquad \text{(Eq. 4-13)}$$

Here, n! means "n-factorial," which is defined as follows:

$$n! = n * (n - 1) * (n - 2)...(2) * (1) \qquad \text{(Eq. 4-14)}$$

The factorial concept will be better detailed in the next section.

As an example of combinations, let's look at the following example. I have a collection of ten books, and I'm about to go on a long trip. I only have room for three books. How many book combinations are there? For this question, we have a set of ten items ($n = 10$) and we are seeking a subset of size three ($r = 3$). Using our combinations formation from Eq. 4-13, we can determine that there are 120 possible book combinations.

4.5.3   Permutations

Combinations are insensitive to ordering. For our book example above, we calculated how many possible combinations there are of size three from ten total items. These 120 combinations are insensitive to any sort of order. For example, books "A," "B" and "C" are the same as books "C," "A," and "B." For permutations, however, we *are* sensitive to ordering. A permutation is a unique ordering from a set of n items, when we take a subset of r items. Notation for permutations is similar to that of combinations – we use $_nP_r$ and $P(n, r)$ to mean the same thing. From a mathematical perspective, the number of unique permutations for a subset of size r from a set of n items is as follows:

$$\text{Permutations} = P(n, r) = \frac{n!}{(n-r)!} \qquad \text{(Eq. 4-15)}$$

As an example of permutations, consider a combination lock with a dial, having forty digits. There is a 3-digit combination to this lock, and the three digits must be unique. We have a set of size forty, and a subset of size three. Using equation 4-15, we have 59,280 unique combinations. If you give the matter serious thought, the term "combination lock" is inappropriate – a "permutation lock" is more appropriate because ordering of the three digits is important.

4.5.4   Excel "Counts"

Fortunately, Microsoft Excel can help us with these combinatorial calculations. While the formulae presented above are helpful in making the appropriate calculations, Excel simplifies the process with the functions shown in Table 4.4.

Excel Function	Purpose
=product(*data range*)	The product of all items in the data range
=factorial(*n*)	*n!*, or "*n*-factorial"
=combin(*n, r*)	$C(n, r)$ or $_nC_r$
=permut(*n, r*)	$P(n, r)$, or $_nP_r$

Table 4.4. Combinatorial Functions in Excel

4.6 Bayes' Theorem

The last section of probability relates to Bayes' Theorem or Bayes' Rule. In its simplest form, Bayes' Theorem gives us the ability to "invert" the components of a conditional probability. Mathematically, this is done as follows:

$$P(A|B) = \frac{P(B|A)P(A)}{P(B)} \qquad \text{(Eq 4-16)}$$

The equation above allows us to "switch" P(B|A) to P(A|B) assuming we know the values of P(B|A), and both P(A) and P(B). Sometimes (perhaps more often than not) the value of P(B) is not directly provided. In this case we must modify the above equation, and generalize, to the following:

$$P(A_i|B) = \frac{P(B|A_i)P(A_i)}{\sum_{k=1}^{n} P(B|A_k)P(A_k)} \qquad \text{(Eq 4-17)}$$

Here, the denominator sums to P(B).

As an example, consider Covid and Covid testing. Let's assume that a person has a 4% chance of having the Covid virus. Furthermore, it has been determined that there is a 75% chance that a person with Covid will test positive for the virus. Finally, there is a 90% chance that a person not having Covid will test negative for the virus. This is all the information we need to determine the probability of someone having Covid when they test positive.

Let's reconcile what we know. Because there is a 4% of a person having Covid (P(Covid) = 0.04), we know there is a 96% probability of a person not having Covid (P(~~Covid~~) = 0.96). We also know that a person with Covid will test positive with a 75% probability (P(+|Covid) = 0.75). This means that a person with Covid will test negative with a 25% probability (P(-|Covid) = 0.25). Finally, we are told that there is a 90% probability that a person without Covid will test negative (P(-|C̶o̶v̶i̶d̶) = 0.90). This means there is a 10% probability that a person without Covid will test positive (P(+|C̶o̶v̶i̶d̶) = 0.10). We can call this a "false-positive." These details have been organized into the following image.

Figure 4.4. Probability Tree for Covid Problem

Note the calculations in red – these detail the probability of a positive test. Mathematically, we have the following:

$$P(+) = P(+|Covid)P(Covid) + P(+|\overline{Covid})P(\overline{Covid}) \qquad \text{(Eq 4-18)}$$
$$= 0.03 + 0.096 = 0.126$$

Similarly, the green cells show us the probability of a negative test is determined as follows:

$$P(-) = P(-|Covid)P(Covid) + P(-|\cancel{Covid})P(\cancel{Covid}) \qquad \text{(Eq 4-19)}$$
$$= 0.01+0.864 = .874$$

This is how the denominator is determined for equations 4-16 and 4-17. So the original question asked the probability of having Covid when a test is positive. In the context of Eq. 4-16, we have the following

$$P(Covid|+) = \frac{P(+|Covid)P(Covid)}{P(+)} \qquad \text{(Eq 4-19)}$$

This reduces to 0.03/0.126, which is 0.2381.

As another example consider a scenario where three machines are producing a manufactured good. Machine A produces 20% of them, Machine B produces 30% of them, and Machine C produces 50% of them. Items made on Machine A have a 5% chance of being defective. Items made on Machine B have a 3% chance of being defective, and items made on Machine C have a 1% chance of being defective. If a randomly selected item is defective, what is the probability it is made on Machine A?

The probability tree below illustrates the scenario. The probability of an item being defective if $P(D) = .01 + .009 + .005 = .024$. These calculations are details in the red cells. Similarly, the probability of an item not being defective is $P(\cancel{D}) = .19 + .291 + .495 = .976$. These calculations are detailed in the green cells. The probability of a randomly selected defective item made on Machine A is as follows:

$$P(A|D) = \frac{P(D|A)P(A)}{P(D)} = \frac{.01}{.024} = .4167 \qquad \text{(Eq 4-20)}$$

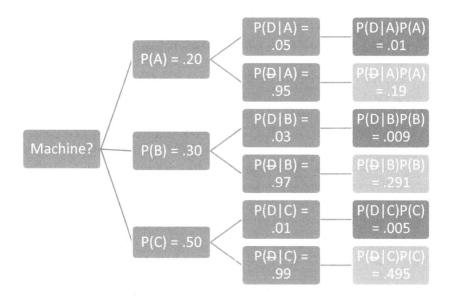

Figure 4.5. Probability Tree for Machine/Defect Problem

4.7 Conclusions

As stated earlier, combinatorics and counting are topics that usually do not find coverage in introductory statistics books. In my opinion they are important because they tell us how many outcomes are possible, which is the "denominator" in probability calculations. Often this number is surprisingly large, which in turn reduces probability. Having this information is valuable, and can be helpful in any sort of organization have a better understanding of the environment in which they operate.

4.8 Exercises

1. I roll a pair of dice. Generate a table showing all possible outcomes and the probability of each outcome.
2. From the table above, what is the probability of rolling either a five or a nine?
3. Are the outcomes from Exercise 1 mutually exclusive? Why or why not?
4. Are the outcomes from Exercise 1 independent? Why or why not?

5. From a standard deck of 52 cards, what is the probability I draw a card of the Spades suit?
6. From a standard deck of 52 cards, what is the probability I draw a ten?
7. Using your answers from problems 5 and 6, what is the probability you draw a 10 of Spades? Does this answer make sense?
8. From a standard deck of 52 cards, what is the probability I draw a five or six?
9. Tonight the Houston Astros play at the New York Yankees. Analysts give the Yankees a 59% chance of winning. The Chicago Cubs play at the Pittsburgh Pirates tonight as well. Analysts project Pittsburgh winning with a 55% probability. Ties are not allowed – a team will either win or lose the game. Using this information, what is the probability that both the Yankees and the Cubs win tonight?
10. Using the information from Exercise 9, what is the probability that either Houston or the Cubs win?
11. Using the information from Exercise 9, what is the probability that neither the Yankees nor Pirates will win?
12. I recently collected some data about people's preference between retailers Wal-Mart and Target. 103 men preferred Target while 67 men preferred Wal-Mart. 158 women preferred Target while 27 preferred Wal-Mart. Using this information, what percent of those surveyed preferred Target?
13. Using the information from Exercise 12, what percent of those surveyed were men?
14. Using the information from Exercise 12, what percent of those surveyed were women that preferred Wal-Mart?
15. Using the information from Exercise 12, of all women, what percent preferred Target?
16. Using the information from Exercise 12, what percent were men given those that preferred Wal-Mart?
17. Can you draw any general conclusions from the information in Exercise 12?
18. If the Yankees and the Red Sox play a four game series, with the Yankees having a 54% of winning each game, generate a histogram showing the probabilities of Yankees wins over the four game span.
    a. What is the probability the Yankees go winless?
    b. What is the probability the Yankees win at least one game?
    c. What is the probability the Yankees sweep the Red Sox?

19. Given the pizza data in Table 3.3, how many pizza toppings are possible if up to two toppings were permitted? Assume double-toppings on any single item (such as double pepperoni) is not permitted.
20. Given the pizza data in Table 3.3, how many pizza toppings are possible if up to two toppings were permitted? Assume double-toppings on any single item (such as double pepperoni) are permitted.
21. I have 15 photos. I have been asked to submit 4 of them for a family photo album. How many photo combinations are possible?
22. I have to visit 10 cities exactly once. The city from which I start my tour must the city in which I end my tour. How many different tours are possible?
23. I am giving an exam to 100 students. I am giving awards to the first, second and third place scorers. How many award scenarios are possible?
24. Every 10 years, there is a McMullen Family Almanac. For the upcoming volume, I have been asked to submit four photos, three recipes, and two short stories. I have ten photos, nine recipes and five short stories to choose from. How many possible combinations can I submit?
25. The New England Patriots played the Philadelphia Eagles in the 2018 Super Bowl. There was a 54% chance New England would win the game. Prior to the game, I was planning on attending the annual Super Bowl party at my friend's house, and I knew there was going to be food served – there was a 35% chance ribs would be served; a 30% wings would be served; a 20% chance pizza would be served and a 15% Chinese food would be served. We will assume that there is no interrelationship between the game's outcome and the cuisine enjoyed at the party. Using this information, what is the probability that either pizza of Chinese food will be served?
26. Using the information from Problem 25, what is the probability that Philadelphia wins and ribs are not served?
27. Using the information from Problem 25, what is the probability that New England wins and either Pizza or Wings is served?
28. Using the information from Problem 25, what is the probability that New England loses and ribs are not served?

29. Using the information from Problem 25, what is the probability that New England wins or ribs are served?

30. Using the information from Problem 25, what is the probability that neither Philadelphia wins, nor are wings served?

31. There is an 0.10% probability a person suffers from a rare form of cancer. A person suffering from this rare form of cancer has an 80% chance of testing positive. Also, a person not suffering from this rare form of cancer has a 99% chance of testing negative. What is the probability of person having this rare type of cancer when they test positive? What is the probability of a false-positive?

32. A truth serum given to a suspect is known to be 90% reliable when the person is a criminal and 99% reliable when the person is not a criminal. If the suspect was selected from a group of suspects where 5% have committed a crime, and the serum indicates he is guilty, what is the probability the suspect is not a criminal?

33. A city has set speed traps at four locations throughout town. The speed traps in the four locations "rotate", and are active with probabilities of 40% for Location 1, 30% for Location 2, 20% for Location 3, and 10% for Location 4. The probabilities of speeding through these four locations are 20%, 10%, 50% and 20% respectively. What is the probability the motorist will receive a speeding ticket?

34. Using Problem 33, what is the probability a person given a ticket drove through Location 1?

35. Using Problem 33, what is the probability a person given a ticket drove through Location 2?

36. Using Problem 33, what is the probability a person given a ticket drove through Location 3?

37. Using Problem 33, what is the probability a person given a ticket drove through Location 4?

5. Random Variables

Probability and statistics can be described in many ways. Dealing with uncertainty is one aspect of the science. There are things in nature of which we never know with certainty. The closing daily stock price of a company, the monthly sales of a specific chemical and legal issues can all be considered sources of uncertainty. We refer to these types of things as **random variables**. Random variables are entities having values that we don't know with certainty. Perhaps we have a general idea of their behavior, but we cannot say with certainty what the outcome will be.

Consider a company's stock price. Today the company's stock price is $10/share. It seems reasonable to think that at this time tomorrow, the company's stock price will be similar to what it is today – perhaps slightly less than $10/share, perhaps slightly more than $10/share. The stock price at the end of a day's trading can be thought of as a random variable. Our hope is to gain an understanding of the random variable in terms of expectation and variation, so that we can make more informed strategic decision regarding all matters related to the random variable of interest.

This chapter evaluates the different types of random variables and describes their properties.

5.1 Discrete Random Variables

A discrete random variable has a finite number of outcomes, and these possible outcome values are known. Consider the roll of a pair of dice. The smallest possible outcome is a two (a pair of ones), and the largest possible outcome is a twelve (a pair of sixes). In total, there are eleven possible outcomes. Each possible outcome has some probability of occurring, and we assume that these probabilities are known.

5.1.1 Discrete Distribution

A specific outcome value of a discrete distribution is referred to as x, and the probability of x occurring is $P(x)$. These probabilities are known. The number of possible outcomes is n. The expected value of a random variable ($\mu = E(x)$), and its standard deviation ($\sigma = \text{std}(x)$) are determined as follows:

$$\mu = E(x) = \sum_{i=1}^{n} x_i P(x_i) \quad \text{(Eq. 5-1)}$$

$$\sigma = \text{std}(x) = \sqrt{\sum_{i=1}^{n}(x_i - \mu)^2 P(x_i)}, \quad \text{(Eq. 5-2)}$$

where x_i represents the value of outcome i. It is also worth noting that the cumulative probability through the ith possible outcome $\Sigma P(x_i)$ is simply the following:

$$\Sigma P(x_i) = \sum_{j=1}^{i} P(x_j) \quad \text{(Eq. 5-3)}$$

Consider an example where a middle-school kid sells newspapers downtown before school. He sells the papers by the "bundle." Any given day he can sell as few as no bundles (x = 0) and as many as six bundles (x = 6). Table 5.1 shows the possible outcomes along with the associated probabilities and cumulative probabilities:

Bundles Sold	P(x)	$\Sigma P(x_i)$
0	.02	0.02
1	.08	0.10
2	.20	0.30
3	.35	0.65
4	.25	0.90
5	.07	0.97
6	.03	1.00

Table 5.1. Newspaper Sales Probabilities

Using the above equations, the kid can expect to sell 3.06 newspapers with a standard deviation of 1.22 newspapers. Figure 5.1 shows both the probability distribution and cumulative probability distributions for the seven possible outcomes. The cumulative probability distribution can be interpreted by stating the associated outcome *or less* has a probability of occurring equal to that particular cumulative probability value. For example, the cumulative probability value of 0.90 is associated with four bundles sold. This means that there is a 0.90 probability that 4 bundles or less will be sold.

Figure 5.1. Probability and Cumulative Distribution of Newspapers Sold

5.1.2   Binomial Distribution

The binomial distribution is a special type of discrete distribution. For each trial, the binomial distribution will result in one of two possible outcomes. The flip of a coin is binomial – either heads or tails will be the result. Consider a stock price – at the end of the day, the stock price will either gain value, or it will not gain value. Using the binomial distribution properties, we can model some specific number of successes (k) over some number of trials (n) given the probability of success (p). Once we know the value of p, we can use its complement to determine the probability of not having success (q, which is 1 - p).

There is a formula available to us that helps us determine the probability of k of successes given a binomial distribution over n trials, with a probability of success, p. The formula is as follows:

$$P(k) = \frac{n!}{(n-k)!k!} p^k q^{n-k}$$ (Eq. 5-4)

Clearly, the above formula is intimidating. The combinatorial object preceding the probability shows the number of combinations of k successes, given the probability of success, p. Fortunately, Excel has a built-in function to perform the probability calculation for k successes over n trials of a binomial distribution. This function is as follows: "=binom.dist(k, n, p, FALSE)," where "FALSE" asks for the probability values – "TRUE" asks for the cumulative probability values.

Let us consider an example of the human resources variety. A human resources manager is evaluated by senior management. Part of the performance review is based upon the tenure of the hires under her leadership. A hire is considered a "success" if they stay with the company for three or more years. As such, at the annual review of the HR manager, the hires from three years earlier are examined – if a hire from three years ago is still with the company it is considered a success. Otherwise, the hire is considered unsuccessful. Generally speaking, there is a 65% probability that a hire from three years ago is still with the company. Let's consider ten hires from three years ago (n = 10). Using the binomial distribution function, the probabilities of "successful" hires from three years ago are as follows:

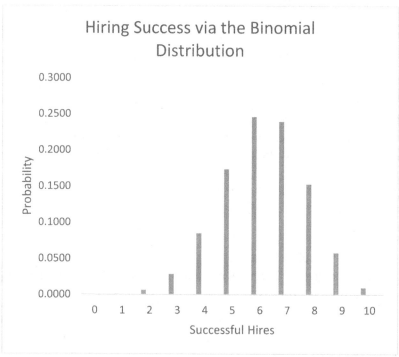

Figure 5.2. Binomial Distribution Example

From Figure 5.2, we can see details of the probability of successful hires from three years ago. From this table, cumulative and inverse cumulative distribution functions can be determined to ask additional questions.

5.2 Continuous Random Variables

The probability distributions described above have a finite number of outcomes. Continuous probability distributions have an infinite number of possible outcomes. While there are many probability distributions to consider, we will examine the uniform distribution and the normal distribution.

5.2.1   Uniform Distribution

The uniform distribution has some minimum possible value, and some maximum possible value. All values between these two extreme values are equally likely to occur.

The random number generator on your calculator is an example of a uniform distribution. When you ask for a random number, you will get some number between 0 and 1. The number will never be less than 0 nor greater than 1. Using the "=rand()" function in Excel will produce the same result. If we generated an infinite number of random numbers via our calculator or in Excel, our histogram would look like this:

Figure 5.3. Uniform Distribution of a Simple Random Number Generator

Note that Figure 4.3 shows all values between 0 and 1 to occur with equal probability.

In truth, the uniform distribution is rarely seen to occur in nature, and is therefore, rarely studied. Its main value is we can simulate scores from a uniform distribution as an input to simulating more complex distributions, such as the normal distribution.

5.2.2   Exponential Distribution

The exponential distribution is mainly concerned with intervals between events. Arrivals are most often studied via the exponential distribution. Given a rate of λ arrivals per time unit (such as minutes), we can understand the probabilities of the amount of time between arrivals. The density function for the exponential distribution, with a time parameter t is as follows:

$$f(t) = \lambda e^{-\lambda t} \qquad\qquad \text{(Eq. 5 - 5)}$$

This equation only helps us with the shape of the distribution. In Excel, the following function is used:

$$f(t) = \text{EXPON.DIST}(t, \lambda, \text{FALSE}) \qquad\qquad \text{(Eq. 5 - 6)}$$

The cumulative density function tells us the probability of an interarrival time

(time between arrivals) being less than t. Mathematically, this is as follows:

$$f(t < T) = 1 - e^{-\lambda t} \qquad \text{(Eq. 5 - 7)}$$

Here, T is some specific value. The Excel version of the equation above is as follows:

$$f(t < T) = \text{EXPON.DIST}(t, \lambda, TRUE) \qquad \text{(Eq. 5 - 8)}$$

Given that λ is the average arrival rate, $1/\lambda$ is the average amount of time that elapses between arrivals. Consider an example where people arrive to a Wal-Mart on a Saturday afternoon at a rate of 3 arrivals per minute. This translates into 1/3 arrivals per minute, or alternatively, 20 seconds between arrivals. Using the Excel formulae above, the density function is as follows:

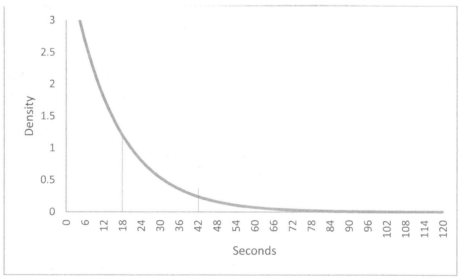

Figure 5.4. Exponential Distribution with $\lambda = 3$

The density function above shows the exponential distribution for $\lambda = 3$ arrivals per minute. If we wish to determine the probability of less than 0.3 minutes (18 seconds) elapsing between arrivals, we can use EXPON.DIST(0.3, 3, TRUE) to learn that this occurs with a 59.34% probability. That is, 59.34% of the area under the curve above is to the left of the vertical line associated with 18 seconds.

If we wish to determine the probability of interarrival time being between 42 and 18 seconds, we use the following relation:

$$p(18 < t < 42) = p(t < 42) - p(t < 18) \qquad\qquad (5\text{-}9)$$

This provides us with 87.75% - 59.34% = 28.41%. The built-in EXPON.DIST function always returns the area to the left of t when using the cumulative distribution.

It should be noted that the amount of time (t) used as an input to the EXPON.DIST function must be in the same time units as those associated with the arrival rate (λ). If λ is given in arrivals per minute, then time units must also be in minutes.

5.2.3 Normal Distribution

The normal distribution is the most important distribution of all. It is often seen in nature. We witness the normal distribution all of the time. The distribution of someone's height or weight, distribution of test scores, the distribution of how much sleep someone got last night, etc. To speak frankly, the normal distribution is a powerful force in nature – the distribution of many things follow a normal distribution. In plotting the normal distribution, the independent variable is "z," the number of standard deviations from the mean. The dependent variable is f(z), the probability, or density function associated with z. In more practical terms, "z" can be thought of as an outcome, whereas f(z) can be thought of as the probability associated with that particular outcome. The mathematical relationship between z and its density function is as follows:

$$f(z) = \frac{1}{\sqrt{2\pi}} e^{\frac{-z^2}{2}} \qquad\qquad \text{(Eq. 5-10)}$$

Clearly, this is a complex calculation. Fortunately, Excel can help us generate a normally distributed plot via the function "=norm.dist(μ, σ, z, FALSE)," where μ is the population mean, σ is the population standard deviation, z is the given z-score, or number of standard deviations from the mean, and "FALSE" asks for the density function, or probability function as opposed to the cumulative density function ("TRUE").

Figure 5.5. The Normal Distribution

The above formula provides us with a z-score, which can then be used to determine probabilities.

It is important to ask probabilistic questions when given a mean and standard deviation of a normally distributed population. The z-score, or number of standard deviations some given value x is from the population mean, μ, is given as follows:

$$z = \frac{x - \mu}{\sigma}$$ (Eq. 5-11)

This formula "standardizes" the normal distribution to having a mean of 0 and a standard deviation of 1. The resultant z-score simply provides the distance between x and μ in units of standard deviations.

This z-score can then be used to determine the area under the curve to the "left" of z, or more specifically, the area under the curve between -∞ and z, which is the integral of Eq. 5-9. Eq. 5-9 cannot be integrated by conventional means, so a numerical method must be used. Fortunately, Excel has provided a function for this. The "normsdist(z)" function provides the area under the normal curve to the left of the z-score. Figure 5.6 illustrates this, where "*p*" represents the area to the left of the z-score.

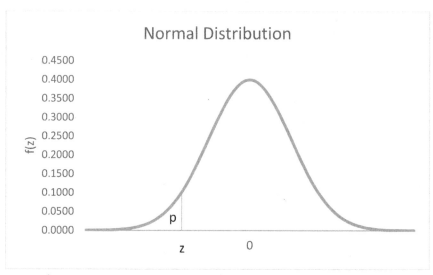

Figure 5.6. z-scores Associated with the Normal Distribution

For example, if we have an exam score having a population mean of 83 with a standard deviation of 5, an exam score of 87 would result in a z-score of 0.80, and an area under the curve of "normsdist(0.80)," which is 0.7881. In other words, the students with scores of 87 did better than 78.81% of the students in the population, also implying they did worse than (100% - 78.81%) 21.19% of the students on the exam.

Conversely, we might also wish to know the exam score associated with some specific percentile. There are tools available to help us with this calculation. First of all, the "normsinv(p)" function returns the z-score associated with the area under the curve equal to p, where the area is to the left of the z-score. Once we have the z-score, we can use Eq. 5-12 to get the actual value x associated with the z-score.

$$x = \mu + z\sigma \qquad \text{(Eq. 5-12)}$$

Of course, this equation is simply a re-arrangement of Eq. 5-11, where we solve for some specific value x.

Continuing with the same example as before, suppose we are interested in finding the exam score associated with the 75th percentile. This would mean the area under the curve, p, is 0.75, and the normsinv(p) function returns a z-score of 0.6745. Using this z-score along with a μ of 83 and a σ of 5, Eq. 5-12 gives us an x of 86.37.

5.3 The Central Limit Theorem

A large part of the remainder of this book relates to gathering sample data from a larger population. When we do this, we are attempting to say something interesting about the population as a whole. It just so happens that the distribution in which we sample most often resembles a normal distribution. This is the essence of the **Central Limit Theorem**. The Central Limit Theorem basically states that when we sample from a population, our findings resemble a normal distribution, and with larger sample sizes, the distribution becomes more defined and more accurately represents the population's distribution.

Figure 5.6 below shows this graphically. Panel (a) shows a histogram as the result of sampling from a population with a sample size of $n = 10$. Panel (b) shows the histogram as the result of sampling from the same population with a sample size of $n = 100$. Panels (c) and (d) show the same, but with sample sizes of 1,000 and 10,000. As one can see, increasing the sample size better resembles the population, providing us with less "predictive error."

Figure 5.7a. Sample Size n = 10

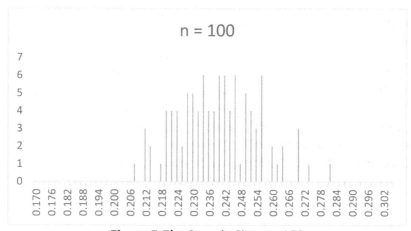

Figure 5.7b. Sample Size n = 100

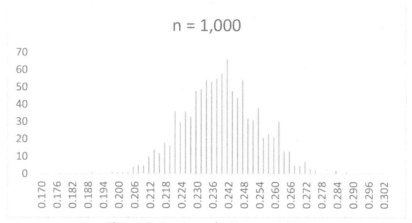

Figure 5.7c. Sample Size n = 1,000

Figure 5.7d. Sampling Size n = 10,000

The "predictive error" as stated above is a bit nebulous. It intends to describe our general ability to understand the population. As one can see from Figure 5.6, larger sample sizes are better in helping us understand the population. We can quantify this phenomenon via the standard error measurement:

$$\text{Standard Error (se)} = s/\sqrt{n}, \tag{Eq. 5-13}$$

where s is the sample standard deviation, and n is the sample size. As one can see, our standard error decreases with larger sample sizes.

The standard error is used to quantify the **sampling distribution**. The sampling distribution is a normal distribution, but is adjusted for the sample size we are using. The t-statistic is used to represent the distance between our sample mean ($\bar{x}$) and the a priori population mean (μ) in units of standard errors. Mathematically, this is as follows:

$$t = \frac{\bar{x} - \mu}{s/\sqrt{n}}$$

(Eq. 5-14)

This particular equation has no application at this point in the book, but it will when we explore hypothesis testing. At this point, it is reasonable just to understand that the t-statistic is the result of sampling, and its value simply represents how many standard errors our sample mean is from the population mean.

5.4 Generating Random Variables

Given the distributions we have studied, it is sometimes desirable to "simulate" values that behave according to pre-specified distributions. That can be accomplished via Excel's built-in random number generator along with other built-in Excel functions. This section provides a short tutorial on how to generate outcomes from specific distributions.

5.4.1   Discrete Distribution

One of the simplest distributions to simulate is the dice roll example. To accomplish this, the RANDBETWEEN function can be used. Specifically, the function generates a value between *min* and *max* via the following command:

RANDBETWEEN(*min, max*)   (eq. 5-15)

This function will return a value between min and max, where min and max are included as possible outcomes. One caveat is that all possible outcomes must be integer. Another caveat is that the probabilities of all outcomes are equal. For more sophisticated discrete distributions, other approaches are needed.

5.4.2   Uniform Distribution

Perhaps the most important simulation tool provided by Excel is the RAND() function. This function returns a value between 0 and 1, which is uniformly distributed – all values between 0 and 1 are equally likely to occur. This distribution is of the continuous variety – an infinite number of possibilities. This function by itself is not particularly help by itself, but when combined with other functions becomes a powerful tool.

To generate a uniformly distributed random variable between *min* and *max*, the following will work:

$$min + (max - min) * \text{RAND}() \qquad\qquad \text{(Eq. 5-16)}$$

5.4.3   Exponential Distribution

Generating a value from the exponential distribution is also possible. With an arrival rate of λ, we can simulate possible interarrival times via the following:

$$-\ln(1 - \text{RAND}()) / \lambda \qquad\qquad \text{(Eq. 5-17)}$$

Here, "ln" is the natural log function.

5.4.4   Normal Distribution

Given that the normal distribution occurs quite often in nature, it is probably the most important distribution to simulate. We will simulate values from the normal distribution via the random normal deviate, which was covered earlier in this chapter. This is done via the "z-score," which is as follows:

$$z = \frac{x - \mu}{\sigma} \qquad\qquad \text{(Eq. 5-18)}$$

As a reminder, the z-score is the number of standard deviations (σ) that lie between the value of x and the population mean (μ). Given that here was are interested in simulating values of x given values of μ and σ, we solve the above equation for x, which is as follows:

$$x = \mu + z\sigma \qquad \text{(Eq. 5-19)}$$

In order to simulate a value of x, we need to use the given values of μ and σ and simulate a value of z. This is done via embedding the RAND() function inside the NORMSINV() function. This yields the following:

$$x = \mu + \text{NORMSINV(RAND())}\sigma \qquad \text{(Eq. 5-20)}$$

As a final note regarding the generation of random numbers, it should be noted that whenever the "F9" key is pressed, EXCEL will re-calculate, and a new random number will be generating, forcing all subsequent calculations to update.

5.5 Conclusions

Despite the fact that many different types of probability distributions were covered in this chapter, we have only scratched the surface in terms of the multitude of probability that exist in nature. Fortunately, the normal distribution is a powerful force in nature, and this particular distribution serves us well for the remainder of this book.

Additionally, the discrete distributions also occur frequently and we now have the ability to better understand them.

5.6 Exercises

1. I roll a pair of dice. What is the expected value of the outcome?
2. I roll a pair of dice. What is the standard deviation associated with the outcome?

Use the information provided in Problem 3 below to address questions 3 – 7.

3. I buy 16 tropical fish of the species "cichlisoma negrofasciata." I cannot determine the gender of the fish, but I'm told there is a 53% probability of a single fish being a female. Construct the appropriate probability distribution, with outcomes of 0 females to 16 females.
4. What is the probability of there being six or fewer females?
5. What is the probability of there being more than nine females?
6. What is the expected number of females?

7. What is the standard deviation of the number of females?

Use the following information to address questions 8 – 12. The population of American males have an average height of 70 inches, with a standard deviation of 1.5 inches.

8. What is the probability of a male having a height of 72 inches or more?
9. What is the probability of a male being 68 inches or shorter?
10. What is the probability of a male being between 69 and 71 inches?
11. What height is associated with the 85th percentile?
12. What height is associated with the 25th percentile?

Use the following information to address questions 13 – 17. On a Saturday afternoon, customer arrive to a theme park once every fifteen seconds.

13. What is the average arrival rate in units of arrivals per minute?
14. What is the average interarrival time in terms of minutes between arrivals?
15. What is the probability that four seconds or less will elapse between arrivals?
16. What is the probability that more then eight second will elapse between arrivals?
17. What is the probability that between ten and twenty seconds will elapse between arrivals?

6. Estimation

We have stated many times that statistics involves using sample data to say things about the population. This will be said many more times before you finish this book. This adage is especially true in this chapter. Here, we wish to articulate a population characteristic based on sample data. Given that we are saying something about the population with incomplete data, we are taking a leap of faith, so to speak. In short, we are *estimating* a population parameter. However, the **confidence interval** helps us articulate how confident we are in our estimate of this particular population parameter.

6.1 Means

Estimating the population mean (μ), via sample data is the first order of business. When we gather sample data, we know the sample size (n), and we can calculate the sample mean ($\bar{x}$) and sample standard deviation (s). We can use this data, along with the appropriate t-statistic to construct a confidence interval, providing a lower bound (*LB*) and an upper bound (*UB*) of our estimate of μ. When this boundary is established, we state a certain level of confidence that the true population mean lies within the specified boundary. The level of confidence we have in this interval, or boundary is 1 - α, where the value of α is either given or assumed. The value of α it typically referred to as the **level of significance** and is an input into the size of the boundaries of the interval. Mathematically, this interval is as follows:

$$P(LB \leq \mu \leq UB) = 1 - \alpha \qquad \text{(Eq. 6-1)}$$

In essence, Eq. 5-1 is telling us that we are (1 - α) confident that the true population mean is between the lower and upper boundaries. We can re-write Eq. 5-1 so that the statistics associated with our sample data are shown:

$$P(\bar{x} - t_{\alpha/2}\frac{s}{\sqrt{n}} \leq \mu \leq \bar{x} + t_{\alpha/2}\frac{s}{\sqrt{n}}) = 1 - \alpha. \qquad \text{(Eq. 6-2)}$$

Here, the value of $t_{\alpha/2}$ represents the distance, expressed via the number of standard errors, our boundary is from the population mean. The $t_{\alpha/2}$ value is often called the **critical value**. This value, multiplied by the standard error, is often referred to as the "**half-width.**" Excel provides us the $t_{\alpha/2}$ value via the following function:

$$t_{\alpha/2} = \text{t.inv.2t}(\alpha, n - 1) \qquad \text{(Eq. 6-3)}$$

This particular value is also used in hypothesis testing for means, covered in the next chapter.

For convenience, the lower and upper boundaries are often shown in the following compressed notation:

$$\bar{x} \pm t_{\alpha/2} \frac{s}{\sqrt{n}} \qquad \text{(Eq. 6-4)}$$

Here, the "±" symbol show that we are both subtracting and adding the margin of error (half-width) from and to our sample mean, $\bar{x}$.

As an example, let's assume that we are interested in a 95% confidence interval estimate of a company's annual salary increases to their employees. We do not have salary increase information for the entire payroll, so we need to randomly select workers and ask them about their annual salary increase. Our random sampling effort resulting in 25 participants ($n = 25$), resulting in a sample mean of an $1,800 annual increase, with a standard deviation of $475. Because we are seeking a 95% confidence interval, our value of $\alpha = 0.05$. Using the appropriate Excel function as shown in Eq. 6-3, we have a $t_{\alpha/2}$ value of 2.06. Substituting these values into Eq. 6-4, we have the following:

$$1,800 \pm (2.06) \frac{475}{\sqrt{25}} \qquad \text{(Eq. 6-5)}$$

This results in a lower bound of $1603.93 and an upper bound of $1996.07. We can then formally state our findings as follows:

$$P(\$1603.93 \le \mu \le \$1996.07) = 0.95 \qquad \text{(Eq. 6-6)}$$

In words, this is stated as follows: *we are 95% confident that our true population mean salary increase is between $1603.93 and $1996.07.*

6.2 Proportions

We can also estimate proportions via confidence intervals. In this context, a **proportion** is the percent of a sample that meets some criterion.

Proportions are often used in understanding consumer preferences, as well as in political science, where we try to gain a better understanding of where candidates stand in terms of voters.

To estimate proportions, we must first define a few terms, which are provided in Table 6.1.

Term	Explanation
$\hat{p}$	Estimate of the population proportion
p	Population Proportion
n	Sample Size
$z_{\alpha/2}$	Critical Value

Table 6.1. Values for Proportion Confidence Interval

The confidence interval for proportions is very similar to that of the confidence interval for means. We add and subtract the standard error times the half-width to and from the estimate. The standard error is as follows:

$$se = \sqrt{\frac{\hat{p}(1-\hat{p})}{n}}$$

(Eq. 6-7)

Using notation similar to that from Eq. 6-4, our confidence interval is as follows:

$$\hat{p} \pm z_{\alpha/2}\sqrt{\frac{\hat{p}(1-\hat{p})}{n}}$$

(Eq. 6-8)

The similarities between Eq. 6-8 and Eq. 6-4 are pretty obvious, but there is one major difference that needs to be discussed. The confidence interval for means exploits a t-distribution because we are sampling from a population – this seems consistent with what was discussed in Section 5.3. The confidence interval for a proportion, however, exploits a z-distribution, despite the fact that we are sampling from a population – this seems counter-intuitive.

The reason that we exploit a z-distribution instead of a t-distribution for a proportion confidence interval is because we assume a large sample size for a proportion confidence interval, which would force t-scores to essentially equal z-scores. It has also been discovered that confidence for proportions are only reliable for larger sample sizes, hence the reason for using the z-distribution.

The z-score that provides us with the critical value for a proportion confidence interval is provided by the following Excel function:

$$z_{\alpha/2} = \text{normsinv}(1-\alpha/2) \qquad \text{(Eq. 6-9)}$$

Let's look at an example of how to construct a confidence interval for a proportion. Let's assume that we administered a taste-test to a group of 1,572 people. Of the people sampled, 832 of them preferred Brand A over Brand B. This means that the estimated proportion of people who preferred Brand A over B is $\hat{p}$ = 832/1572, which equals 0.5292. If we desire a 99% confidence interval, then α = 0.01. Using Eq. 6-9 to obtain the z-score, we have $z_{\alpha/2}$ equal to 2.5758. Substituting these values into Eq. 6-8, we the following confidence interval:

$$P(0.4968 \leq p \leq 0.5617) - 0.99 \qquad \text{(Eq. 6-10)}$$

Another way of saying the above is that there is a 99% probability that the true proportion of consumers preferring Brand A over B is between 0.4968 and 0.5617.

6.3 Differences Between Means

The last type of confidence interval we cover is the confidence interval for the difference between two means. Here, we are actually sampling from two populations and constructing a confidence interval based upon the differences in their expected values. For this exercise, we introduce some new, but familiar terms in Table 6.2.

Quantity	Sample 1	Sample 2
Sample Size	n_1	n_2
Population Mean	μ_1	μ_2
Sample Mean	$\bar{x}_1$	$\bar{x}_2$
Sample Standard Deviation	s_1	s_2

Table 6.2. Values Used for Difference Between Means Confidence Interval

The standard error for this confidence interval is as follows:

$$se = \sqrt{\frac{s_1^2}{n_1} + \frac{s_2^2}{n_2}} \qquad \text{(Eq. 6-11)}$$

The degrees of freedom are as follows:

$$df = \frac{\left(\frac{s_1^2}{n_1} + \frac{s_2^2}{n_2}\right)^2}{\left(\frac{1}{n_1 - 1}\right)\left(\frac{s_1^2}{n_1}\right)^2 + \left(\frac{1}{n_2 - 1}\right)\left(\frac{s_2^2}{n_2}\right)^2} \qquad \text{(Eq. 6-12)}$$

The formula for the confidence interval of the difference between two population means is as follows:

$$(\bar{x}_1 - \bar{x}_2) \pm t_{\alpha/2} \sqrt{\frac{s_1^2}{n_1} + \frac{s_2^2}{n_2}} \qquad \text{(Eq. 6-13)}$$

Here, the $t_{\alpha/2}$ value is the same as it was as stated in Eq. 5-3.

As an example, let us construct a 90% confidence interval ($\alpha = 0.10$) for the difference in average exam scores administered to two different classes. The following data is provided:

Quantity	Sample 1	Sample 2
Sample Size	$n_1 = 47$	$n_2 = 52$
Sample Mean	$\bar{x}_1 = 81$	$\bar{x}_2 = 83.5$
Sample Standard Deviation	$s_1 = 7.2$	$s_2 = 6.2$

Table 6.3. Example Data for Difference in Average Exam Scores

Using the given values and formulae, our confidence interval is as follows:

$$P(-4.76 \le \mu_1 - \mu_2 \le -0.24) = 0.90 \qquad \text{(Eq. 6-14)}$$

In other words, the difference in population means between the two classes is between -4.75 and -0.25.

6.4 Sample Size Determination

We use α to assist us in determining the width of our confidence interval. We can modify this calculation to determine the sample size needed to provide a pre-specified level of confidence, given a pre-specified interval width, for our estimate.

6.4.1   Sample Size for Single Population Mean Estimates

As stated earlier, we know that the confidence interval for a mean from a single population is as follows:

$$\bar{x} \pm t_{\alpha/2}\frac{s}{\sqrt{n}} \qquad \text{(Eq. 6-15)}$$

The part of this that we subtract from, and add to the sample mean can be referred to was the "half-width," noted by $W/2$. The above equation can then be re-written as follows:

$$\frac{W}{2} = t_{\alpha/2}\frac{s}{\sqrt{n}} \qquad \text{(Eq. 6-16)}$$

When this equation is re-arranged and solved for the sample size (n), we have the following:

$$n = \left(\frac{t_{\alpha/2}s}{W/2}\right)^2 \qquad \text{(Eq. 6-17)}$$

Because our critical value of $t_{\alpha/2}$ is a function of the unknown sample size n and α, we generalize and use the following:

$$n = \left(\frac{z_{\alpha/2}s}{W/2}\right)^2 \qquad \text{(Eq. 6-18)}$$

As an example, we extend our earlier example, where we derived the following mean estimate: $P(\$1,603.93 \leq \mu \leq \$1,996.07) = 0.95$. Using the same value of s ($475), when we desire a 95% level of confidence with an interval width of $300 ($W/2 = \$150$), we would have the following:

$$n = \left(\frac{(1.96)(475)}{150}\right)^2 = 38.52 \qquad \text{(Eq. 6-19)}$$

As such, we would need a sample size of 38.52 units to achieve a 95% confidence interval with a width of $300.

6.4.2 Sample Size for Proportion Estimates

As is the case with estimated means, we can determine the sample size for will provide a specified level of confidence given a specified interval for a population proportion. Consider the confidence interval for a proportion estimate:

$$\hat{p} \pm z_{\alpha/2}\sqrt{\frac{\hat{p}(1-\hat{p})}{n}} \qquad \text{(Eq. 6-20)}$$

The part we add to, and subtract from, the proportion estimate ($\hat{p}$) is once again referred to as the "half-width," and is denoted by W/2. The above equation then becomes:

$$\frac{W}{2} = z_{\alpha/2}\sqrt{\frac{\hat{p}(1-\hat{p})}{n}} \qquad \text{(Eq. 6-21)}$$

Re-arranging the equation and solving for the sample size (n) results in the following:

$$n = \frac{\hat{p}(1-\hat{p})}{\left(\frac{W/2}{z_{\alpha/2}}\right)^2} \qquad \text{(Eq. 6-22)}$$

As an example, we re-visit the brand-preference problem, where 832 of 1572 people preferred Brand A over Brand B, using $\alpha = 0.01$. To achieve an interval width of 0.05 (W/2 = 0.025), we require a sample size of 2,644.87:

$$n = \frac{0.5292(1-0.5292)}{\left(\frac{0.025}{2.58}\right)^2} = 2{,}644.87 \qquad \text{(Eq. 6-23)}$$

6.5 Conclusions

Generating confidence intervals is simply a way to estimate values associated with a population. The more confident we need to be, the wider the interval must be. As the same time, if we use as a large a sample size as possible, the width of our intervals with narrow.

Problems of this type become very helpful when we pursue two-tailed tests of hypotheses in the next chapter. Because of this, the next chapter, which has substantial content is eased a bit because of this chapter.

6.6 Exercises

1.   The "NFLLinemen" data set contains data on the weight of randomly sampled offensive lineman in the National Football League. Using $\alpha = 0.01$, construct the appropriate confidence interval for the population mean.

2.   Using $\alpha = 0.05$, construct a confidence interval on the pulse rates of randomly selected university athletes. The data set is provided in the "PulseRate" file.

3.   I randomly sampled 2,234 North Carolinians on whether or not they considered Wake Forest University the best school in the state. 1,465 respondents did consider Wake Forest the best school in the state. Construct a 95% confidence interval to estimate the true proportion of those who think Wake Forest is the best school in the state.

4.   3,689 Oregonians were randomly asked if they support legalization of marijuana for medicinal purposes. 2,983 people responded in the affirmative. Using this data to construct a 93% confidence interval to estimate the true proportion of Oregonians that support legalization of marijuana for medicinal purposes.

5.   Professor Fraud and Professor Quick both teach separate sections of Principles of Finance. They gave the same exam to the students. The "FinanceProfessors" data set provides the exam scores for both sections. Use this data to construct a 90% confidence interval on the difference between the two sections.

6.   Is one professor better than the other? Why or why not?

7. A food company just came up with two new products for diabetics: Product X and Product Y. They are concerned about the amount of carbohydrates in the product, as diabetics need to be careful about carbohydrate intake. The file "DiabeticFoods" contains carbohydrate data (in grams) for randomly selected items of the two different products. Construct a 96% confidence interval for the difference in carbohydrates between the two products.

8. Regardless of the type of confidence interval constructed, what does a wide confidence interval suggest?

9. Regardless of the type of confidence interval constructed, what does a narrow confidence interval suggest?

10. What is the margin of error in Problem 3?

11. What is the margin of error in Problem 4?

7. Hypothesis Testing

In science or commerce, we are not permitted to make unsubstantiated claims. For example, if I work for an electronics firm, I cannot tell my colleagues and managers the following: "our Q55 electronic switches cannot handle a 25-volt load." What is wrong with this question? We have made a claim without any evidence of formal scientific testing. In order to make a reasonable claim outside of a pub, we need to support the claim with scientific proof of the claim's authenticity. To provide the scientific proof, we need to conduct a formal hypothesis test.

This chapter provides us the tools to make hypothesis tests. We will test hypotheses involving means, proportions and differences between means. In other words, we extend the work from the previous chapter with the intent of affirming a disproving a claim.

7.1 General Process

A hypothesis is a **claim**, **inference** or **conjecture**. These terms are used interchangeably. Chapter 6 of this book is called "**Hypothesis Testing**," while other books might use "**Statistical Inference**." Regardless of the terminology used, we are testing a claim about the population to see if it is supported by scientific proof. Determining whether or not a claim is true requires a formal hypothesis test.

These tests take on three different types. The first type of test is interested in whether or not a population parameter is equal to some specific value vs. *not equal to* some value. The second type of test is concerned with determining whether or not some population parameter is equal to some value vs. *less than* some value. The third type of test is concerned with whether or not some population parameter is equal to some value vs. *greater than* some value. These three types of tests are formalized in the subsequent sections.

7.1.1   Null and Alternative Hypotheses

Each hypothesis test involves two different hypotheses: the **null hypothesis (H_0)** and the **alternative hypothesis (H_A)**. These two hypotheses are stated at the same time.

The null hypothesis test is a benign hypothesis and states the status quo – it states what is typically regarded as true. Here is an example of a null hypothesis: the average weight of a box of Cheerios is 14 ounces. Mathematically, we would state this as follows:

$$H_0: \mu = 14 \qquad \text{(Eq. 7-1)}$$

Note that the population mean is involved in H_0. This is the case because the H_0 is making a claim about the population. Also note that equality is involved – the H_0 will always involve equality, because we are claiming the status quo. Finally, we should note that when making our conclusions about a hypothesis, we always base our conclusion on the H_0: we will either *reject* H_0, or *fail to reject* H_0.

The alternative hypothesis, H_A, contradicts H_0. H_A says something of interest involving inequality. H_A is typically the direct question in which the researcher/investigator is most interested. As stated earlier, there are three types of H_A: one that states "not equal to;" one that states "less than;" and another stating "more than." The H_A is where the "burden of proof" lies. H_A must provide evidence beyond a reasonable doubt that the H_0 is incorrect. If a criminal trial comes to mind via this description, you are definitely on the right track: we assume H_0 is true (innocence) unless proven otherwise (guilt is proven beyond a reasonable doubt). This brings us to potential errors. As is the case with a criminal trial, we can make mistakes in our decision regarding H_0. A Type I Error occurs with the probability of α, while the probability of a Type II Error occurs with the probability of β. Table 7.1 explores these possible errors.

	Reject H_0	Do Not Reject H_0
H_0 True	Type I Error	Correct Decision
H_0 False	Correct Decision	Type II Error

Table 7.1. Outcomes from H_0 Decisions

The first type of H_A we discuss is the "not equal to" variety. When presented alongside H_0 in our Cheerios example, we have the following:

$$H_0: \mu = 14; H_A: \mu \neq 14 \qquad \text{(Eq. 7-2)}$$

Not equal to implies inequality – we do not specifically consider which type of inequality (neither "<" nor ">"). One might wonder who might be interested in this scenario. One possible answer, in the context of this example, would be the quality control people who make the Cheerios. They simply wish to consistently fill the boxes with 14 ounces of cereal. Figure 7-1 shows this scenario graphically with regard to the population mean. The shaded areas are referred to as the "reject regions." Because the H_A states "not equal to," we have a "<" reject region and a ">" reject region. Because we have reject regions on both sides of the distribution, we call this a "two-tail test."

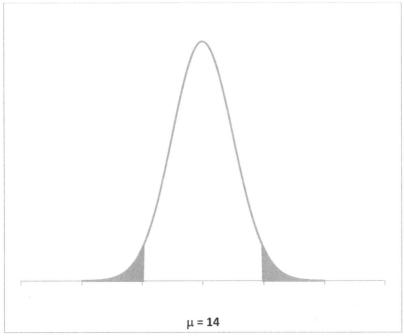

$\mu = 14$

Figure 7-1. H_0: $\mu = 14$; H_A: $\mu \neq 14$

The second type of H_A is the "less than" hypothesis. In the context of our Cheerios example, we would say the following:

$$H_0: \ \mu = 14; \ H_A: \ \mu < 14 \tag{Eq. 7-3}$$

For this example, an interested party might be consumer advocates who wish to expose Cheerios for "skimping" on the amount of Cheerios they put into their boxes, in the event that H_A is true. Figure 7-2 graphically shows this scenario, with the reject region on the left-hand side. Because we have reject region on just one side of the distribution, we call this a "one-tail test."

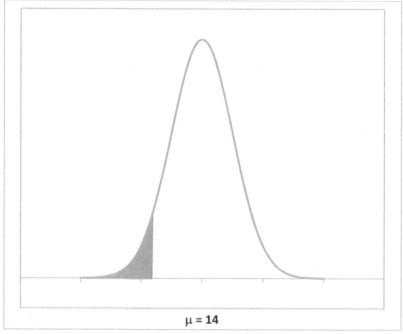

$\mu = 14$

Figure 7.2. H_0: $\mu = 14$; H_A: $\mu < 14$

The last type of H_A we explore is the "greater than" scenario. Continuing with our Cheerios example, we have the following:

$$H_0: \mu = 14; H_A: \mu > 14 \qquad \text{(Eq. 7-4)}$$

For this particular scenario, senior executives at General Mills (the company who makes Cheerios) might be interested because if H_A were true, cereal would be given away, which is an unforgivable offense in the eyes of senior management and shareholders. Figure 7-3 shows this scenario, where you will note the reject region is on the right hand side. Because we have reject region on just one side of the distribution, we call this a "one-tail test."

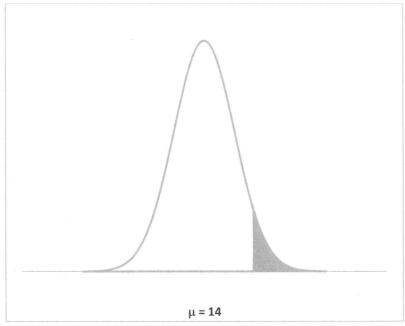

$$\mu = 14$$

Figure 7-3. H_0: $\mu = 14$; H_A: $\mu > 14$

With the general concepts of H_0 and H_A now stated, it is time to discuss the steps of hypothesis testing.

7.1.2   Steps of the Hypothesis Test

Students often consider hypothesis testing the most difficult aspect of statistics – that was certainly the case for me. However, with practice (and a good teacher), the following steps of the process become second nature.

7.1.2.1   Constructing H_0 and H_A

Properly constructing H_0 and H_A are the most difficult part of the process. It is important to note that the instructor has a very large responsibility here in clearly writing the questions. Have a look at the following hypothetical questions:

a)   The quality control department at Cheerios is concerned about putting 14 ounces of cereal into the boxes. If they put too few Cheerios into the box, customers are not getting their money's worth. If they put too much cereal into the boxes, General Mills loses money. As such, putting 14 ounces of cereal into the boxes is supremely important. Using the "Cheerios" data set, please determine if General Mills is putting the proper amount of cereal in the boxes.

b) The DeliveryGuys parcel service claims a delivery time of less than 6 hours. Using the "DeliveryGuys" data set, please determine if their claim is true.

c) CircuitKings makes circuit boards for TV remote controls. They use a silver alloy for conductivity. Each circuit board should contain .25mg of the silver alloy. If more than this amount of the alloy is used, CircuitKings loses money because the silver alloy is very expensive. CircuitKings is worried that they are putting too much of the alloys in their circuit boards. Using the CircuitKings data set, please determine if they are putting too much silver alloy in their circuit boards.

Each of these statements are fair and clearly written. Statement "a" should result in H_A being of the "$\neq$" variety, because the dangers of putting too little cereal into the box is just as bad as putting too much cereal into the box. Statement "b" should result in H_A being of the "<" variety because a direct claim is made implying as much. In this case, the H_A is explicitly stated, which occasionally happens. Statement "c" is of the ">" variety because the dangers of putting too much of the silver alloy is discussed. In summary, then, we have the following hypotheses ready for testing:

a) H_0: $\mu = 14$; H_A: $\mu \neq 14$
b) H_0: $\mu = 6$; H_A: $\mu < 6$
c) H_0: $\mu = 0.25$; H_A: $\mu > 0.25$

There are two important rules to remember here. First, the H_0 always involves equality – writing H_0 is easy. Second, the H_A always involves inequality. Another important thing to remember is that the H_A is more interesting than the benign H_0. A final noteworthy item is that if you find the problem not clearly written, where the "inequality" is vaguely worded, a "$\neq$" H_A is probably the best choice.

For this section, we will use scenario "a" above as our example:

$$H_0: \mu = 14; H_A: \mu \neq 14$$

Additionally for this example, we will use $\alpha = 0.05$, and the Cheerios data set, which contains 25 observed weights of randomly-selected Cheerios boxes claiming to be 14 ounces.

7.1.2.2   Defining the Reject Region

When performing hypothesis testing, you will either be given a value of α or you will need to assume one. Typically, on homework assignments and exams, α should be given. On written assignments of a "case-based" nature, it is reasonable to have the student assume a value of α. The value of α determines the size of the reject region – it is as simple as that. If α is small, then the reject region is small. If α is large, then the reject region is large. In figures 7-1 – 7-3, the values of α are represented by the shaded areas, which comprise the reject region. We use the "t.inv" functions in Excel to obtain the critical value associated with α. Inputting α and the degrees of freedom (df) in the t.inv function, we get an output of the critical value, defining the reject region.

H_A Type	Excel Function
$\neq$	+/- t.inv.2t(α, n-1)
<	t.inv(α, n-1)
>	t.inv(1-α, n-1)

Table 7.2. Excel Functions for Reject Regions

This critical value will be compared with the test-statistic (discussed next) to determine whether or not H_0 should be rejected.

Regarding our example, we use $\alpha = 0.05$ and t.inv.2t(0.05, 25 - 1), which results in a critical value of +/- 2.06. This value is both positive and negative because we are seeking a critical value for both tails.

There is one final comment that needs to made about the value of α. Students often ask what value of α should be used. This is a good question. A rule of thumb is to use $\alpha = 0.05$, but this varies across industries. The medical industry often uses value of 0.01 or lower. Lower values of α result in more conservative tests, while higher values of α result in more liberal tests. What this means is that conservative tests make it harder to reject H_0, while more liberal tests make it easier to reject H_0. If seeking a more liberal test, however, an α value exceeding 0.10 is considered inappropriate. Never use an α value in excess of 0.10.

7.1.2.3   Determining the Test Statistic

The critical value is compared to the test statistic. The test statistic is the result of the following formula, which was introduced in Chapter 6:

$$t = \frac{\bar{x} - \mu}{s/\sqrt{n}} \qquad \text{(Eq. 7-5)}$$

From the Cheerios data set, we have the following statistics: the sample mean ($\bar{x}$) is 14.03, with a sample standard deviation (s) of 0.1087. The data set contains $n = 25$ observations. We also have, of course, our hypothesized population mean of $\mu = 14$. Substituting these values into Eq. 7-5, we have the following test-statistic:

$$t = \frac{14.03 - 14}{0.1087/\sqrt{25}} = 1.51 \qquad \text{(Eq. 7-6)}$$

This value of 1.51 tells us that our sample mean is 1.51 standard errors above the hypothesized population mean. It is above the hypothesized population mean because it has a positive sign – in other words, $\bar{x}$ exceeds μ.

This test statistic is compared to the critical value, so that we can make a decision regarding H_0.

7.1.2.4   Decision Regarding H_0

As stated earlier, we compare the critical value(s) with the test statistic. Figure 7.4 shows the result of our test in a graphical sense. You will notice that our test statistic does not fall into the reject region – the shaded area. Because of this, we DO NOT reject H_0. As such, we do not have adequate evidence to say anything contrary to H_0. General Mills is in fact putting 14 ounces of cereal into the boxes. If the test statistic did fall into the reject region, we would reject H_0, and claim that General Mills is not putting 14 ounces of cereal into the boxes.

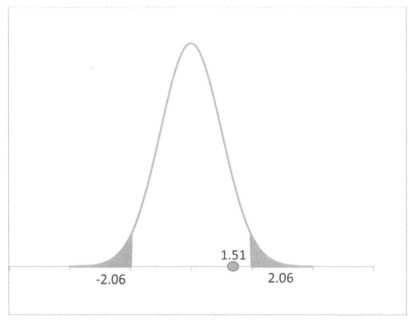

Figure 7.4. Results of Example Hypothesis Test

7.1.2.5 Calculating the p-value

The p-value of the test is the last thing we need to calculate. The p-value is the size of the reject region associated with the test statistic. Figure 7.5 shows us the p-value from a visual perspective.

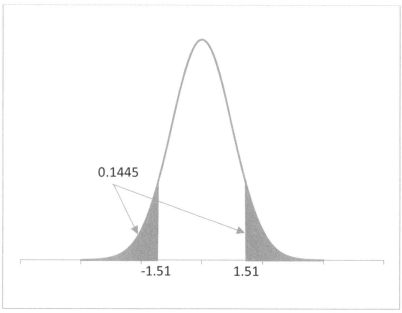

Figure 7.5. The p-value Associated with the Example Hypothesis Test

Because this is a two-tailed test, we must make the shaded region associated with the test-statistic two-tailed as well. In order for us to calculate the p-value, we must use the tdist functions, which are detailed in Table 7.3.

Number of Tails	Function
1-Tailed Test	tdist(|t|, n-1, 1)
2-Tailed Test	tdist(|t|, n-1, 2)

Table 7.3. Functions for p-value.

You will note that the p-value is greater than the value of α. This should be the case because we failed to reject H_0. If our test statistic found itself in the reject region, we would reject H_0, and our resultant p-value would be less than our value of α. If we already knew that we weren't going to reject H_0 in this example, why did we calculate the p-value? The answer to this question is because the p-value gives us more information – it tells us the "break-even" value that could be used for α – the point of indifference between rejecting and not rejecting H_0. If p is less than α, we reject H_0. If p is greater than α, we fail to reject H_0. Or more crudely put:

If the p is low, H_0 must go. If the p is high, H_0 will fly.

Comparisons between the p-value and α are not intended to confuse the student. I have noticed over the years that the adage above puts things in proper perspective for students. The p-value is more important than α, because the p-value can be compared to any threshold (α). In fact, statistical software packages don't even ask for values of α – they just return p-values. Figure 7.6 shows JMP output for our example problem – you will only see a p-value reported, nothing about the value of α.

Figure 7.6. p-value Calculation via JMP

While not completely true from a technical standpoint, I like to think of the p-value of the test as the probability that the H_0 is true.[2]

7.2 Testing Means

Of course, the example problem we explored throughout the previous section was a test concerning means. There are also tests concerning proportions and differences between means. In this section, we will do another hypothesis test involving means.

For this example problem, we will consider the DeliveryGuys example,

---

[2] More specifically, the p-value is defined as *the probability of obtaining a result more extreme than what was observed, assuming H_0 is true*. "More extreme" means further into the reject region. It is my opinion it is reasonable to consider the p-value the probability of H_0 being true.

described in the previous section. As you recall, DeliveryGuys claim an average delivery time of less than six hours. This results in the following:

$$H_0: \mu = 6; H_A: \mu < 6$$

We will use the DeliveryGuys data set, containing $n = 40$ observations, and we will assume an $\alpha = 0.01$. Our descriptive statistics tell us that the sample mean ($\bar{x}$) is 5.89, and the sample standard deviation (s) is 0.2836. The hypothesized population mean is, of course, $\mu = 6$. Using t.inv(0.01, 40-1), we have a critical value of -2.43. Using Eq. 6-6 to calculate the t-statistic, we have the following:

$$t = \frac{5.89 - 6}{0.2836/\sqrt{40}} = -2.45 \qquad \text{(Eq. 7-7)}$$

Since the t-statistic is more extreme than the critical value, we reject H_0 and claim a delivery time of less than 6 hours. Figure 7-7 shows the relationship between the critical value and the test statistic.

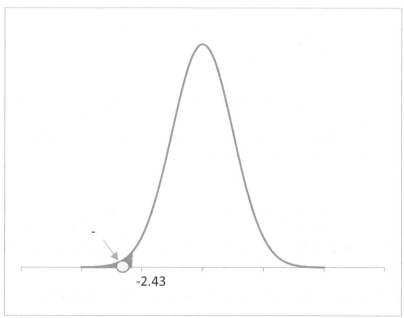

-2.43

Figure 7-7. Result of One-Tail Hypothesis Test

The test statistic falls into the reject region. Using the tdist function to calculate the p-value, we have the following:

$$\text{p-value} = \text{tdist}(|-2.45|, 40 - 1, 1) = 0.0094 \quad\quad \text{(Eq. 7-8)}$$

Note that our p-value above is less than $\alpha = 0.01$, supporting our decision to reject H_0.

It should be noted that Eq. 7-8 takes the absolute value of the t-statistic as an argument, because this function will return an error message if the t-statistic is negative. This caveat is also noted in Table 7-3.

7.3 Testing Proportions

The second type of hypothesis test we discuss relates to proportions: whether or not sampling provides us a value equal to some hypothesized value. As was the case with testing means, there are three different types of H_A: not equal to, less than and greater than. Unlike testing means, for testing proportions, we use the z-distribution instead of the t-distribution. The reason for this is because for testing proportions, we always assume a large sample size, rendering the t-distribution the same as the z-distribution. Because of this, our critical values, given some value of α are shown in Table 7-4.

H_A Type	Excel Function
$\neq$	+/- normsinv(1 - α/2)
<	normsinv(α)
>	normsinv(1 - α)

Table 7.4. Excel Functions for Proportion Test Reject Regions

Note that for the two-tailed test, our critical value takes on both +/- values. As a reminder from our coverage of confidence intervals for proportions, "$\hat{p}$" is our sample proportion, while "p" represents the true population proportion. Given this, our test statistic is shown in Eq. 7-9

$$z = \frac{\hat{p} - p}{\sqrt{\frac{\hat{p}(1 - \hat{p})}{n}}} \quad\quad \text{(Eq. 7-9)}$$

With the basic formulae in place, let's explore an example problem. Hank and Keenan are running for mayor of Louisville, Kentucky. The winner of the election will receive a majority of the votes – more than 50% of the vote to be specific. 352 people have been sampled, and 182 of them have voted for Keenan. At the $\alpha = 0.03$ level, can we conclude that Keenan is the winner?

This problem essentially asks if Keenan has more than 50% of the vote, which is our H_A. As such, we have the following:

$$H_0: p = 0.50; H_A: p > 0.50 \qquad \text{(Eq. 7-10)}$$

Because this is a one-tailed test, our critical values is "normsinv(1 - 0.03)," which is 1.88. Our value of $\hat{p}$ is 182/352 = .5170. This provides us with a test statistic of

$$z = \frac{0.5170 - 0.50}{\sqrt{\dfrac{0.5170(1 - 0.5170)}{352}}} = 0.64 \qquad \text{(Eq. 7-11)}$$

The test statistic does not fall into the reject region, so we fail to reject the H_0, as we do not have sufficient evidence to claim Keenan as the winner. Figure 7-8 shows this graphically:

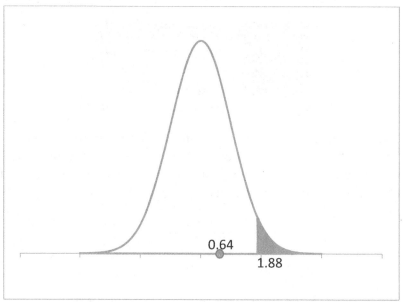

Figure 7-8. Results of Mayoral Election

In terms of the p-value for this type of test, we use the "normsdist" function. Depending on the type of H_A, we use the following functions:

H_A Type	Excel Function
$\neq$	2*(normsdist(-|z|))
<	normsdist(z)
>	1 − normsdist(z)

Table 7.5. Excel Functions for Proportion Test p-values

For this problem, our p-value is then $1 - \text{normsdist}(0.64)$, which is 0.2611.

The above problem brings up an issue that is relevant to everyday life. If you watch the news regarding politics and elections, you will see lots of polling. If you look at the details of the polling, you will sometimes see something like a "margin of error of +/- 3.5%." This "margin of error" that is referred to is simply what we call the standard error, $\sqrt{\hat{p}(1 - \hat{p})/n}$. Smaller sample sizes result in larger "margins of error," which should make sense given what we have already learned about the central limit theorem.

Let us consider one other example. In the hot dog business, the USDA places an upper limit on variety meats that can be put into hot dogs. "Variety meats" are tongues, tails, snouts, etc. Hot dogs must have less than 5% variety meats. A local hot dog maker decides to test whether or not they are in compliance. They documented their last 200 batches, and found an average of 1.5% variety meats in them. At the $\alpha = 0.05$ level, are they in compliance?

Clearly, our hypotheses are as follows: H_0: $p = 0.05$; H_A: $p < 0.05$. Using normsinv(0.05), we have a critical value of -1.65 which defines the reject region. Using Eq. 7-9, our test statistic is as follows:

$$z = \frac{0.015 - 0.05}{\sqrt{\dfrac{0.015(1 - 0.015)}{200}}} = -4.07 \quad \text{(Eq. 7-12)}$$

This test statistic is very small, and is in an extreme part of the reject region. When normsdist(-4.07) is used to find a p-value, a very small number may appear. In my case the number displayed was "2.33E-05." This means $(2.33)(10)^{-5}$, which a very small number. When this happens, we simply state that p < 0.0001.

7.4 Testing Differences Between Means

There are times when we need to determine whether or not means from two different populations are the same. Additionally, there are times when we need to determine whether or not there is a *specific* difference in means from two different populations. We can do this via hypothesis testing. Before showing the appropriate calculations, we refresh your memory with some relevant terms.

Quantity	Sample 1	Sample 2
Sample Size	n_1	n_2
Population Mean	μ_1	μ_2
Sample Mean	$\bar{x}_1$	$\bar{x}_2$
Sample Standard Deviation	s_1	s_2

Table 7.6. Values Used for Difference Between Means

When we test from two different populations for equality of means, we can construct the following hypotheses:

$$H_0: (\mu_1 - \mu_2) = 0; \; H_A: (\mu_1 - \mu_2) \neq 0 \qquad \text{(Eq. 7-13)}$$

For a specific different in means, we can use the following, where "d" represents the value of the specific difference:

$$H_0: (\mu_1 - \mu_2) = d; \; H_A: (\mu_1 - \mu_2) \neq d \qquad \text{(Eq. 7-14)}$$

Both sets of hypotheses above are two-tailed tests, but one-tailed tests are also possible, where H_A: is of the "<" or ">" variety, although the one-tailed tests are not as common as the two-tailed tests. As with other tests, we are given or we assume a value for α. Table 7.6 shows the t.inv functions we use to determine critical values for reject regions:

H_A Type	Excel Function
$\neq$	$+/-$ t.inv.2t(α, df)
$<$	t.inv(α, df)
$>$	t.inv($1-\alpha$, df)

Table 7.7. Excel Functions for Reject Regions

Here, the value for degrees of freedom, *df*, is as follows:

$$df = \frac{\left(\frac{s_1^2}{n_1} + \frac{s_2^2}{n_2}\right)^2}{\left(\frac{1}{n_1 - 1}\right)\left(\frac{s_1^2}{n_1}\right)^2 + \left(\frac{1}{n_2 - 1}\right)\left(\frac{s_2^2}{n_2}\right)^2} \qquad \text{(Eq. 7-15)}$$

The *general* test statistic for the difference between means is as follows:

$$t = \frac{(\bar{x}_1 - \bar{x}_2) - (\mu_1 - \mu_2)}{\sqrt{\frac{s_1^2}{n_1} + \frac{s_2^2}{n_2}}} \qquad \text{(Eq. 7-16)}$$

If we are testing for equality in means, Eq. 7-16 simplifies to the following, because equality of population means implies $\mu_1 = \mu_2$:

$$t = \frac{(\bar{x}_1 - \bar{x}_2)}{\sqrt{\frac{s_1^2}{n_1} + \frac{s_2^2}{n_2}}} \qquad \text{(Eq. 7-17)}$$

If we are testing for a specific difference in means equal to "d," where d $= \mu_1 - \mu_2$, then Eq. 7-16 simplifies to the following:

$$t = \frac{(\bar{x}_1 - \bar{x}_2) - d}{\sqrt{\frac{s_1^2}{n_1} + \frac{s_2^2}{n_2}}} \qquad \text{(Eq. 7-18)}$$

The-p-values for these types of tests are similar to that shown in Table 6-3. They are modified here to show degrees of freedom specific to this problem type:

Number of Tails	Function
1-Tailed Test	tdist($|t|$, df, 1)
2-Tailed Test	tdist($|t|$, df, 2)

Table 7.8. Functions for p-value.

Let's do an example using the data set "ExamScores." This data set compares the scores from two different exams administered at a public university with very large classes. Exam 1 was taken before Exam 2. We are interested in seeing if the performances on the two exams were the same at the $\alpha = 0.05$ level. We have the following hypotheses:

$$H_0: (\mu_1 - \mu_2) = 0; \quad H_A: (\mu_1 - \mu_2) \neq 0 \qquad \text{(Eq. 7-19)}$$

The following descriptive statistics are captured from the data set:

Quantity	Exam 1	Exam 2
Sample Size	$n_1 = 500$	$n_2 = 500$
Sample Mean	$\bar{x}_1 = 80.00$	$\bar{x}_2 = 77.00$
Sample Standard Deviation	$s_1 = 4.00$	$s_2 = 6.99$

Table 7.9. Summary Data for Difference in Exam Scores

The data set results in $df = 796.23$. Our critical value is obtained via t.inv.2t(0.05, 796.23) = +/- 1.96, and we have a test statistic of t = 8.33. Because the test-statistic is more extreme than the critical value, we reject H_0, and claim that the performances between Exams 1 and 2 were not the same. Our p-value is obtained via Table 7-8, which is tdist($|8.33|$, 796.23), which is less than 0.0001.

We will do another example of differences between means. Both Alberto and Guillermo are world-class runners, specializing in the 400m dash. Alberto claims that he averages one second faster in the event than does his competitor Guillermo. Using this information, we can construct the following hypotheses:

$$H_0: (\mu_G - \mu_A) = 1; \ H_A: (\mu_G - \mu_A) \neq 1^3 \qquad \text{(Eq. 7-20)}$$

We will use $\alpha = 0.03$. Our data set "Time400m" yields the following statistics:

Quantity	Guillermo	Alberto
Sample Size	$n_G = 13$	$n_A = 15$
Sample Mean	$\bar{x}_G = 45.8s$	$\bar{x}_A = 44.6s$
Sample Standard Deviation	$s_G = 0.23s$	$s_A = 0.18s$

Table 7.10. Summary Data for 400m Times

The degrees of freedom, as determined via Eq. 6-15 is 22.65. Our critical value is t.inv.2t(1 − 0.03, 22.65), which is +/- 2.32. Our test statistic, as determined via Eq. 7-18 is as follows:

$$t = \frac{(45.8 - 44.6) - 1}{\sqrt{\dfrac{0.23^2}{13} + \dfrac{0.18^2}{15}}} = 2.53 \qquad \text{(Eq. 7-21)}$$

Given that our test statistic is more extreme than our critical value, we reject H_0 and claim that Alberto is in fact more than one second faster than Guillermo. As stated in the structure of the actual test statistic, Guillermo is more than one second slower than Alberto. The p-value is tdist(2.32, 22.65, 2) = 0.0189.

7.5 Confidence Intervals and Two-Tailed Test

It is possible that you may have noticed some similarities between the two-tailed test and confidence intervals. This would not be a coincidence – there is a definite relationship. When we construct a confidence interval, we are using the estimated value of expectation (such as $\bar{x}$) to form an interval where we are 1 - α confident the true population lies. This action is very similar to a two-tailed test. In fact, if we construct a confidence interval using

---

[3] Here, Guillermo's hypothesized slower time is subtracting Alberto's hypothesized faster time so as to have a positive value of the test statistic, simplifying understanding We are than essentially saying that Guillermo is more than one second slower than Alberto. Also note that our value of $d = 1$, the hypothesized difference in average time.

some value of α, and that interval contains the hypothesized population parameter (such as μ), we know that we fail to reject H_0 at that particular value of α. Conversely, if the interval does not contain the population parameter, we know to reject H_0 at that specific value of α.

As an example, let's re-visit our Cheerios example. Using the formulae from Section 6.1 and the Cheerios data set, we construct a 95% confidence that is as follows:

$$P(13.99 \leq \mu \leq 14.08) = 0.95 \hspace{2cm} \text{(Eq. 7-22)}$$

One will notice that the hypothesized population mean of 14 *is* included in this interval, telling us that H_0 is not to be rejected. Conversely, if the hypothesized population mean was not in this interval, we would reject H_0.

Because of this unique relationship between confidence intervals, and two-tailed tests, we essentially added value to confidence intervals.

7.6 Conclusions

It is my opinion that hypothesis testing is the most difficult part of learning statistics. It is also my belief that it is the most important part of statistics. Making a proclamation to the world requires a formal test so as to support the proclamation – at least this is true in the scientific community, which is an important community in society. As such, it is imperative that we understand hypothesis testing.

While the topic may be difficult, it is not unreasonably difficult. The most important part is to understand and visualize the H_0 and H_A. Once this is accomplished, the rest falls into place. Of course, practice is needed so that the proper formulae and Excel functions are correctly used in the pursuit of the problems.

7.7 Exercises

For problems involving actual hypothesis testing of data, the following steps are required:

a) State the appropriate hypotheses
b) Report the critical value.
c) Report the test statistic

d) State your decision regarding H_0.
e) Report the p-value.

1. Use the criminal justice system in the US to provide an example of a Type I error.
2. Use the criminal justice system in the US to provide an example of a Type II error.
3. Mike Trout of the Anaheim Angels thinks his batting average exceeds 0.320. What are the appropriate hypotheses associated with this claim?
4. Motorola invented the concept of six-sigma – claiming production of less than 3.4 defects per million units produced. What are the appropriate hypotheses associated with this claim?
5. LeBron James claims that when Cleveland plays Chicago in basketball, Cleveland beats them by an average of six points. What are the appropriate hypotheses associated with this claim?
6. Use the "WireGaugeData" set to determine, via hypothesis testing at the $\alpha = 0.05$ level if there is a difference in wire diameter.

7. A courier service advertises that its average delivery time is less than 6 hours for local deliveries. A random sample of times for 12 deliveries to an address across town was recorded. These data are shown below. Is this sufficient evidence to support the courier's advertisement at the 5% level of significance? Delivery time data: 3.03, 6.33, 6.50, 5.22, 3.56, 6.76, 7.98, 4.82, 7.96, 4.54, 5.09, 6.46

8. Mike's Bikes in Columbus, Georgia sells a great many road bikes. One of the things that causes Mike Reynolds (the store's proprietor) heartburn is customers coming back in with tire problems. If too much air is put into the tires, blowouts can occur, which are dangerous. In addition to blowouts, the inner tubes must be replaced, which is difficult. If too little air is put into the tires, poor bike performance results, specifically frequent tire replacement. Mike is wondering if his mechanics are putting the correct amount of air in the tires. The correct amount of air needed for the tires is 115 psi (pounds of air pressure per square inch). Mike randomly sampled 100 inflated tires, and discovered the mean tire pressure to be 113.58 psi, with a

standard deviation of 8.1 psi. At the $\alpha = 0.08$ level, what can we conclude about the tire pressure at Mike's?

9. ThreeGuys Chemical Corporation in Cincinnati has a new sodium nitrate rust inhibitor out. The product (called The MoistureBasher) is marketed as a process additive for machine parts used in high-humidity environments. Three Guys claims that when using the MoistureBasher, machine parts can last for 90 days prior to needing replaced due to rusting. A consumer-advocacy group based in Boston decided to test this claim of ThreeGuys – they believe the rust protection is less than 90 days. They treated 20 machine parts with the MoistureBasher and measured the usable duration of machines parts treated with the product. They found a mean duration of 81 days with a standard deviation of 2.5 days. What does this sample information say about the performance claim of ThreeGuys?

10. Individuals filing Federal Income Tax returns prior to March 31 had an average refund of $1,056. Consider the population of "last minute" filers who mail their returns during the last five days of the income tax period (April 10-15). A sample of 400 late filers was collected, and it was determined that their average refund was $910 with a standard deviation of $1,600. Do late filers receive a refund less than $1,056? Use $\alpha = 0.05$.

11. Ten years ago, the A.C. Nielson service claimed that on average, an American household watched 6.70 hours of television per day. An independent market research group believes that more television is watched now. To test this claim, 200 households were surveyed, and they found a mean of 7.25 hours of television are watched now, with a standard deviation of 2.5 hours. Has the amount of television viewing increased over the last ten years? Use $\alpha = 0.02$.

12. Historically, evening long-distance phone calls from a particular city average 15.2 minutes per call. In a random sample of 35 calls, the sample mean time was 14.3 minutes per call, with a sample standard deviation of 5 minutes. Use this sample information to test for any change in the mean duration of long-distance phone calls. Use $\alpha = 0.02$.

13. A manufacturer of a nylon rope claims that their 10 mm rope withstands a load of more than 250 pounds of force before breaking.

To validate this claim, several ropes were subjected to loads and the force at which they broke was documented. These forces are expressed in pounds, and are as follows: 280, 259, 255, 238, 245, 265, 250, 259, 241 and 260. Use α = 0.06. Is the manufactures claim credible?

14. A large manufacturer of an electronic component claims that their 0.5 V connecter is consistently produced at a rate of less than 10 defective units per million units produced. Sampling has revealed that the last several lots had defects per million units produced as follows: 3, 8, 7, 13, 8, 4, 11, 10, 9, 6, 10 and 8. Is the manufacturer's claim of less than 10 defects per million legitimate? Use α = 0.04.

15. Use the "DiabeticFoods" data set, and perform the appropriate hypotheses.

16. Use the "FinanceProfessors" data set, and perform the appropriate hypotheses.

17. Use the "NFLLinemen" data set, and perform the appropriate hypotheses.

18. Use the "PulseRate" data set, and perform the appropriate hypotheses.

19. Use the data from Problem 5-4. Do a majority of Oregonians support medicinal marijuana?

20. Use the data from Problem 5-3. Do a majority of North Carolinians consider Wake Forest University the best school on the state?

21. Luca Brazzi wishes for the extra-large pizza pies at his pizzeria to have 15 pepperoni slices each. Too few slices result in unhappy customers, and too many slices reduce the profitability of the operation. Luca has randomly sampled several extra-large pizzas and has recorded the number of pepperoni slices on each pizza. This data is included in the "PepperoniSlices" data set. Is the pizzeria putting the appropriate number of pepperoni slices on the pizza? Use α = 0.03.

22. A manufacturer of allergy relief medication claims that they have come up with a pill that provides more than eight hours of allergy relief. Because claims related to the pharmaceutical industry require scrutiny, a value of $\alpha=0.01$ must be used. Several severe allergy sufferers were tested using this medication, and the hours of allergy relief that they gained is reported via the included data set ("AllergyRelief"). Your job is to either validate or refute the pharmaceutical firm's claim.

23. Luca Brazzi's pizzeria also delivers pizza and sandwiches to their Brooklyn-based customers. Luca promises the customers a delivery time of less than thirty minutes. To make sure delivery time is in fact less than 30 minutes, Luca has randomly collected delivery times over the last few months of operation. These data are included in the "PizzaDeliveryTime" data set. Is the delivery time less than 30 minutes? Use $\alpha = 0.06$.

24. The Provost of a prestigious regional college is concerned that freshman students are spending too little time studying. She thinks that freshman students study less than six hours per day. To put this concern to the test, she gathered a small sample of students and asked them to report the hours of study time that they incurred on a single day. The hours of study data are available via the included data set ("StudyTime"). A statistics professor from the mathematics department suggested that the Provost use a value of $\alpha=0.10$ for the test. Your job is to test the veracity of the Provost's claim.

25. The U.S. National Park Service claims that the Old Faithful Geyser in Yellowstone National Park requires an average of 78 minutes between eruptions. To validate this claim, the time between eruptions was measured at random intervals by the U.S. Geological Survey. They measured, in minutes, the time that elapsed from the start of one eruption until the start of the next ("TimeBetweenEruptions"). These measurement values are available via the attached data set. Use a value of $\alpha = 0.05$. Is Old Faithful that "faithful?"

26. A month or so ago, an angry customer complained to Luca Brazzi that the waiting time for a table was too long. The customer told Luca that the waiting time was in excess of 20 minutes during the dinner rush (between 6 and 8 PM). Luca wanted to investigate the angry

customer's claim, so he randomly gathered waiting time data for the dinner rush. This waiting time data is included under the "RestaurantWaitingTime" data set. Is the waiting time in excess of 20 minutes? Use $\alpha = 0.005$.

27. A company in Omaha, Nebraska blends sausage. They use a combination of premium and variety meats in their sausage blends. Variety meats are not as appetizing as their name might suggest – they are comprised of the least desirable parts – tails, tripes, etc. As such, the USDA imposes that sausage blends must be less than 15% variety meats by weight. The Omaha meat packer has collected data from their last several sausage blends. The data set is included under the "Variety Meats" name. Using $\alpha = 0.03$, determine if the meat packer is in compliance with the USDA.

28. Two presidential candidates, named "Hillary" and "Bernie" are running for the Democratic presidential nomination in the Wisconsin Primary. Several voters were randomly selected (upon their exiting the polling places) and asked for whom they voted. The results of this exit polling were collected and are available via the "Wisconsin Primary" data set. A value of "0" indicates no vote for the candidate of interest, while a value "1" indicates a vote for the candidate of interest. It should be noted that for all sampled, their vote was cast for either "Hillary" or "Bernie." Using $\alpha = 0.02$, can we project a winner of the Wisconsin Primary? If so, who do we project as the winner?

29. A pharmaceutical company makes an over-the-counter antihistamine drug that combats basic allergy symptoms. The drug's active ingredient is hydrochloric acid (HCl). HCl is supposed to comprise 2.5% of the drug. If too little HCl is put into the drug, the effect of the drug is diminished. If too much HCl is put into the drug, side effects become more likely. Given these factors, it is important that the drug consistently contain 2.5% HCl. Several recent batches of the drug were studied and the HCl was recorded. This data is available via the "Allergy Drug" data set. It should be noted that all batches used for the sample data set are the same size. Using $\alpha = 0.05$, can the

pharmaceutical company claim that the drug contains the correct amount of HCl?

30. The data set "Monthly Closing Prices" contains closing prices for both Microsoft and IBM on a monthly basis. Perform the appropriate test to determine if the monthly percent change differs between the two stocks. Use $\alpha = 0.05$.

31. SuperPrep helps high school students prepare for the math portion of the SAT test. They claim that their students average more than 100 points better on the SAT math portion as compared to the students of the BasicPrep service. Using $\alpha = 0.05$, and the "SATPrep" data set, determine if their claim is legitimate.

8. Power of Hypothesis Test

In Chapter 7, we emphasized the fact that when we use sample data to make claims about a population, we run the risk of arriving at incorrect conclusions. This is OK – this issue is inevitable, given that we are working with limited information. In the presences of this, we "pre-specify" the probability of making an error. We did this in the form of α, our level of significance.

In this chapter, we will further explore α and its relationship to β, another type of error in hypothesis testing.

8.1 Type I Errors and α

As stated in the last chapter, there are two type of errors associated with hypothesis testing. Table 8.1 reminds us of this:

	Reject H_0	Do Not Reject H_0
H_0 True	Type I Error	Correct Decision
H_0 False	Correct Decision	Type II Error

Table 8.1. Outcomes from H_0 Decisions

Here we are reminded that rejecting H_0 when it is in fact true is called a Type I Error, and occurs with a probability of α. Let us try to visualize this with an example. Suppose we are making chocolate chip cookies and we worry that we are putting more than 15 chips in each cookie. Using a level of significance of $\alpha = 0.05$, we can construct the appropriate hypotheses as follows:

$$H_0:\ \mu = 15;\ H_A:\ \mu > 15 \qquad \text{(Eq. 8-1)}$$

Graphically, we have the support of Figure 7.1 so that we can visualize the issue at hand.

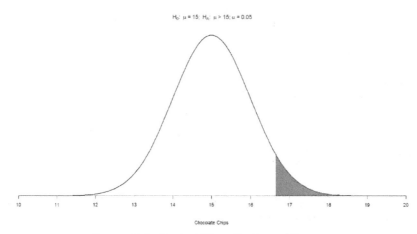

$H_0: \mu = 15; H_A: \mu > 15; \alpha = 0.05$

Chocolate Chips

Figure 8.1. Probability of a Type I Error

The probability distribution is centered at the value of $\mu = 15$. Given that we have specified an α of 0.05, 5% of the area under this curve is in the right-hand tail, which constitutes our reject region. For a large sample size at this specific value of α, our reject region is 1.645 standard errors above the mean. Assuming a standard error of 1 here, we can claim our reject region is defined by 16.645 chocolate chips and above. Again, Figure 8.1 displays this.

Now, let us assume for a moment that the H_0 is in fact TRUE. In other words, we are certain that there are 15 chocolate chips in each cookie. Given that 5% of the area under the curve is in the reject region, we then have a 5% chance of incorrectly rejecting H_0 when it is true. This means that we have a 5% of committing a Type I error.

Understanding a Type II error and its associated probability of β is a bit more complicated than the above.

8.2 Type II Errors and β

A Type II error is committed when we fail to reject the H_0 when it is not true. In order to understand this, we need to visualize the scenario with the help of the alternative hypothesis, H_A. When the H_0 is true, the H_A is false. Conversely, when the H_0 is false, the H_A is true.

8.2.1   Type II Error for ">" Tests

Let's continue with our chocolate chip cookie example, and for sake of argument, let's assume that the H_0 is false, making the H_A true. That is, the H_A is the correct hypothesis. Using the same value of $\alpha = 0.05$ as before, we have the following scenario, where both H_0 and H_A are shown in Figure 8-2.

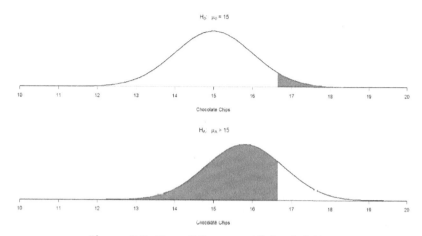

Figure 8.2. Type II Error and β for ">" H_A

Here, the H_0 is the same as before. What is new to this, however, is that the H_A is shown to have a greater mean than H_0. When discussing the Type I and Type II errors, we will use μ_0 and μ_A to represent the population means of H_0 and H_A, respectively. For the top portion of Figure 8.2, the value of α shows the reject region for H_0 – the shaded area on the right hand side of H_0. The critical value here is 16.645 chocolate chips, as discussed above.

When we examine the lower portion of Figure 8.2, the area under the curve on the left hand side of the critical value of 16.645 represents the value of β. That is, β is the area under the H_A curve that corresponds with the "do not reject" region of the H_0. This gets back to the definition of β – the probability of not rejecting H_0 when it is false.

Simply defining β is, in my opinion, not terribly helpful. It must be visualized, given the logic involved.

8.2.2   Type II Error for "<" Tests

As another example, let us consider a test where we are concerned that an allergy medication is providing less than 10 hours of relief. The appropriate hypotheses for this problem would be:

$$H_0: \mu = 10; H_A: \mu < 10 \qquad \text{(Eq. 8-2)}$$

Graphically, we would have the following:

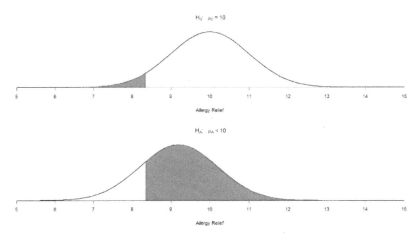

Figure 8.3. Type II Error and β for "<" H_A

Again, we use $\alpha = 0.05$ here, and assume a large sample size resulting in a standard error of 1. The top part of Figure 8.3 shows a reject region defined by left-handed side of H_0 associated with 8.355 (10 – 1.645). The lower part of Figure 8.3 shows that β is defined by the right hand side of H_A, starting at 8.355.

8.2.3   Type II Error for "≠" Tests

When we are confronted with a test of the "≠" variety, we have reject regions in two tails of H_0. This means that when determining β, we inspect the H_A and visualize β as the area between the two critical values associated with H_0. Figure 8-4 shows an example of this, where were are interested in determining whether or not we are consistently putting 35 pounds per square inch (psi) in automotive tires. Our hypotheses are as follows:

$$H_0: \mu = 35; H_A: \mu \neq 35 \qquad \text{(Eq. 8-3)}$$

A graphical representation of these hypotheses and their associated α and β values are as follows:

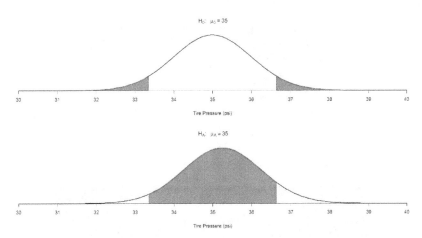

Figure 8.4. Type II Error and β for "≠" H_A

Here, we see that our value of β is the area between the two critical values for the H_0 associated with α.

Most certainly, understanding β is more complex than understanding α. The secret to understanding β is to visualize, and realize that β is the area under the H_A, that would be in the "do not reject" region of H_0. To this point, we have generalized details of our example problems, with the intent being to focus on visualization of β, via the H_A.

8.3 Computing β

Now that we have an understanding of how to visualize β, the obvious question then becomes "how do we compute β?" To do this, we must first have some specific value of the mean associated with the H_A, which we symbolically refer to as μ_A. The value of μ_A can be assumed, but another approach to quantifying it is to use the sample mean that we calculated, $\bar{x}$. Using $\bar{x}$ for this purpose makes perfect sense, as it is a value that is not precisely equal to the value of the mean associated with the H_0, which we refer to as μ_0. Additionally, using $\bar{x}$ is the result of our sampling effort, and therefore, serves as our best possible estimate of the population mean.

To calculate the value of β, we need to first compute a few things. The first thing we need to do is to calculate the critical value for the specific hypothesis test. This critical value, cv, is a function of α, and we learned how to do this in the previous chapter. As a reminder, these details are as follows:

H_A Type	Critical Value (cv)
$\neq$	+/- t.inv.2t(α, df)
<	t.inv(α, df)
>	t.inv(1-α, df)

Table 8.1. Excel Functions for Critical Values

Next, we need to determine the t-statistic that defines β. The following formulae show us how these values are computed.

H_A Type	t-statistic
$\neq$	$t_1 = \left[\mu_0 - cv(s/\sqrt{n}) - \mu_A\right]/(s/\sqrt{n})$ $t_2 = \left[\mu_0 + cv(s/\sqrt{n}) - \mu_A\right]/(s/\sqrt{n})$
<	$t = \left[\mu_0 + cv(s/\sqrt{n}) - \mu_A\right]/(s/\sqrt{n})$
>	$t = \left[\mu_0 + cv(s/\sqrt{n}) - \mu_A\right]/(s/\sqrt{n})$

Table 8.2. Excel Functions for t-statistics

We are finally ready to compute β. To do this, we simply take our t-statistics as determine above and use the "tdist" function in Excel. Specifically, we use the following functions:

H_A Type	β Calculation
$\neq$	(1 - tdist($|t_2|$, n-1, 1))-tdist($|t_1|$, n-1, 1)
<	tdist(t, n-1, 1)
>	tdist($|t|$, n - 1, 1)

Table 8.3. Excel Functions for β values

Of course, the mathematics here are comprehensive – lots of calculations to manage. To alleviate this problem, custom Excel functions have been constructed to make this easier. They are as follows:

H_A Type	β Function
$\neq$	Beta2T(μ_0, μ_A, s, n, α)
<	BetaLeft(μ_0, μ_A, s, n, α)
>	BetaRight(μ_0, μ_A, s, n, α)

Table 8.3. Excel Functions for β values

As stated earlier, the examples in Section 8.2 were very generalized. The intent was not mathematical, but conceptual, so that the probability of a Type II error can be visualized. These conceptual problems were numerically solved via the specific data sets related to the examples above. The Excel data files, descriptive statistics, along with the calculated values of β are shown below. In all instances, the value of μ_A was set equal to the sample mean, $\bar{x}$.

H_A Type	Excel File	μ_0	μ_A	s	n	α	β
$\neq$	TirePressure	35	35.27	2.44	67	0.05	0.8578
<	AllergyReliefHours	10	9.18	2.19	62	0.05	0.1030
>	ChocolateChips	15	15.81	2.03	100	0.10	0.0041

Table 8.4. Values of β for Example Problems

8.4 The "Power" of a Test and the Behavior of β

As we learned previously, the "confidence" of a test is $(1 - \alpha)$. Similarly, the "power" of a test is $(1 - \beta)$. In fact, many refer to β indirectly by simply referring to the "power" of a test. The lower our value of β is, the more powerful our test.

There are two major factors that impact β and the power of our test. First, the larger the difference between our values of μ_0 and μ_A, the smaller our value of β will be. Similarly, the larger our sample size is, the smaller our value of β will be. Again, the smaller our value of β, the more powerful the test.

This difference between the values of μ_0 and μ_A is often referred to as the "gap" and is as follows:

$$\delta = |\mu_0 - \mu_A| \qquad\qquad \text{(Eq. 8-4)}$$

This phenomenon can be illustrated by what we call the operating characteristic (OC) curve, which shows the relationship between the value of δ and the associated value of β.

To illustrate the OC curve, we have selected our "ChocolateChips" example and let the value of μ_A vary between 15 and 17 chocolate chips, resulting δ values ranging from 0 to 2, since the μ_0 value is fixed at 15 chocolate chips. We have constructed the OC curve for three difference sample sizes: n = 25, 100 and 500. This is shown if Figure 8.5 below.

One will clearly notice that larger sample sizes and larger gaps between μ_0 and μ_A will reduce the value of β, and therefore increase the power of our test. Larger sample sizes and larger gaps between μ_0 and μ_A result in steeper curves, which makes for a more powerful test.

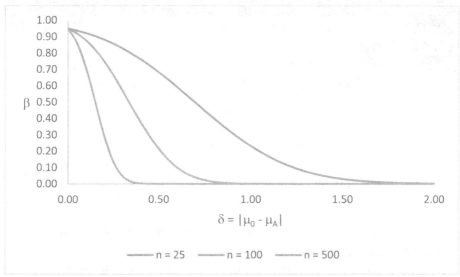

Figure 8.5. Operating Characteristic Curve for "ChocolateChips" Problem

8.5 Choosing the Sample Size

When we perform a hypothesis test, we pre-specify the value of α – the Type I Error risk that we call the level of significance, which indirectly determines the level of confidence we desire with our test. We can also pre-specify the Type II Error risk that also determines the power of our test. When we pre-specify both α and β, we need to calculate the sample size (n) needed to obtain the pre-specified error probabilities. For a one-tail test, this calculation is as follows:

$$n = \left[\left(z_\alpha + z_\beta\right)^2 s^2\right]/\delta^2 \qquad \text{(Eq. 8-5)}$$

For a two-tail test, this calculation is as follows:

$$n = \left[\left(z_{\alpha/2} + z_\beta\right)^2 s^2\right]/\delta^2 \qquad \text{(Eq. 8-6)}$$

For these two equations, the "z-value" is the critical values associated with α and β. These values of z are analogous to critical values quantified by t. But here, we assume a large sample size, which is better generalized by the z-statistic as opposed to the t-statistic. We capture these values of z the same we did for hypothesis tests associated with proportions. Table 8-5 shows us the Excel functions used to find these values.

H_A Type	z_α, or $z_{\alpha/2}$	z_β
$\neq$	normsinv(1 - α/2)	normsinv(1 - β)
<	normsinv(1 - α)	normsinv(1 - β)
>	normsinv(1 - α)	normsinv(1 - β)

Table 8.5. Excel Functions for z-values

As an example, let us once again consider the data set TirePressure data set as described in Table 8.4. For this example, we pre-specify α = 0.05, β = 0.03, δ = 0.25, and from our sample data, we already know that s = 2.44. Given that this is a two-tail test, we use Eq. 8-6, and the functions from Table 8.5 and find that $z_{\alpha/2}$ = 1.96 and z_β = 1.88. Using Eq. 8-6, we have the following:

$$= [(1.96 + 1.88)^2 2.44^2]/0.25^2 = 716.93 \qquad \text{(Eq. 8-7)}$$

As such, in order to have a Type I Error of 0.05 and a Type II Error of 0.03 for this particular problem, we need a sample size of 717 units.

8.6 Conclusions

Very few introductory statistics classes and/or books give much treatment to Type II Errors. As such, this topic is often treated as "optional."

Nevertheless, it does provide more information on the hypothesis test in general, and also illustrates the relationship between potential errors (both Type I and Type II) and the sample size.

8.7 Exercises

For these problems, assume the "gap value" of δ to be $|\mu_0 - \bar{x}|$.

1. What is the value of β, for the hypothesis test associated with Problem 6-7?

2. What sample size should be used if we desire β to be 0.025 for Problem 6-7

3. What is the value of β, for the hypothesis test associated with Problem 6-8?

4. What sample size should be used if we desire β to be 0.05 for Problem 6-8

5. What is the value of β for the hypothesis test associated with Problem 6-9?

6. What sample size should be used if we desire β to be 0.01 for Problem 6-9?

7. What is the value of β for the hypothesis test associated with Problem 6-11?

8. What sample size should be used if we desire β to be 0.04 for Problem 6-11

9. What is the value of β for the hypothesis test associated with Problem 6-12?

10. What sample size should be used if we desire β to be 0.02 for Problem 6-12

11. What is the value of β for the hypothesis test associated with Problem 6-13?

12. What sample size should be used if we desire β to be 0.06 for Problem 6-

13

13. What is the value of β for the hypothesis test associated with Problem 6-14?

14. What sample size should be used if we desire β to be 0.05 for Problem 6-14

9. Simple Linear Regression

We have covered the basic foundations of statistical inference – testing a claim via a formal test, so that we can properly articulate our findings to the skeptical scientific community. This is an important accomplishment. This chapter will build on our ability to do this via exploring potential relationships between variables. We read about exploration between variables in everyday life. For example, we have learned about a relationship between exposure to asbestos and mesothelioma, a type of lung cancer. We have learned about a relationship between the amount of time a child watches television and the likelihood of that child being obese.

These "relationships" are typically implied using very subtle language. Nevertheless, these relationships are almost always determined via some form of linear regression – formally exploring the relationships between variables, or entities. In this chapter, we will cover simple linear regression, which is the exploration between two variables. Many informative and important investigations can be made with just a basic understanding of this powerful tool.

9.1 Slope and Intercept

Prior to delving into regression from a statistical standpoint, it is important for us to recall from high school algebra the formula for a line. The lines has two major components: an **intercept** and a **slope**. The reference system for a line is the Cartesian Coordinate System, where "x" represents the horizontal axis and "y" represents the vertical axis. A point in this coordinate system is represented via "(x, y)" notation. The line has the general formula:

$$y = a + bx \qquad \text{(Eq. 9-1)}$$

Under this scenario, we assume the x-value is pre-determined – we call "x" an **independent variable**. We assume that y-values are determined by the x values – we call "y" a **dependent variable**.

The intercept, represented by "a" is the value of the y-value when "x" equals zero. Graphically, this is where the line crosses the vertical axis (y-axis). The slope, represented by "b" is the ratio of the change in y to each unit change in x. Mathematically, this is often stated as follows:

$$b = \Delta y / \Delta x \qquad \text{(Eq. 9-2)}$$

Figure 9.1 shows a line of the form "$y = 3 + 2x$.

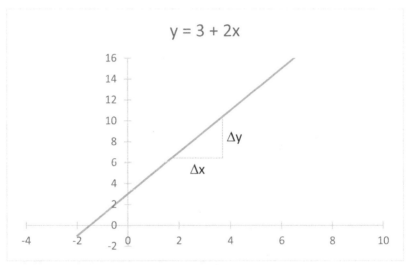

Figure 9.1. Example Linear Model

This example line has an intercept of "3" – notice how the line crosses the vertical axis at $y = 3$ ($y = 3 + 2(0) = 3$). This example line has a slope of "2." The $\Delta y / \Delta x$ ratio is equal to "2" – this is detailed in the "wedged" section of Figure 9.1.

9.2 Ordinary Least Squares Regression

In statistics, we are given a set of data and it is our job to "fit" a line through the points represented by the data set. As an example of a data set, consider a situation where we are interested in exploring the relationship between price and demand of a product. In this example, we have randomly visited convenience stores in Winston-Salem, NC. In each store, we looked at the price of a 12-pack of Diet Dr. Pepper in cans. Management provided us with the sales data for this product in units sold for the previous week. This data set is as follows:

Pr.	3.38	3.42	3.48	3.52	3.55	3.55	3.61	3.61	3.67	3.72
Dem	83	86	83	81	81	83	81	81	80	80

Table 9.1. Price vs. Demand Data for Diet Dr. Pepper

A scatter plot is shown in Figure 9.2.

Figure 9.2. Scatter Plot for Diet Dr. Pepper Demand Data

Here we see points, showing the demand for each price, as the result of our random sampling effort. As one might expect, there seems to be an inverse relationship between price and demand – as price increases, demand seems to increase.

In order to find the "best" line relating price to demand, we select a slope and intercept that minimizes the **sum of squared errors**. Figure 9.2 also shows a fitted line. This fitted line is the result of selecting a slope and intercept that minimizes the total squared difference between the actual data points and the fitted line. These error terms are shown via the thin vertical lines spanning the fitted line and the actual data values. We square these error terms for two reasons: first, to prevent negative numbers; second, to amplify large errors. Statistical software will provide us with a slope and intercept value that minimizes the sum of squared errors. The practice of finding the slope and intercept terms is called "**ordinary least squares regression**."

The next section will detail how to perform ordinary least squares regression in Microsoft Excel, but for our data set, we have a slope of -$14.00 and an intercept of 131.60 units of Diet Dr. Pepper. What this means is that when the price is zero, we can expect a demand of 131.60 units. This result, of course, should not be taken literally, but the intercept is where the line crosses the vertical ("y") axis. The slope tells is that for each $1 increase in the price, we can expect demand to *decrease* 14.00 units. The negative sign tells us it is a decrease.

9.3 Statistical Inference for Slope and Intercept

Here, we continue with our Diet Dr. Pepper example and learn how to use Excel to give us the slope and intercept. Then we test the statistical significance of the slope and intercept.

9.3.1　Excel for Regression

In order to learn the values of the slope and intercept, we use the Data Analysis Tools | Regression option. We enter the data associated with the "x" and "y" values. Again, for our example, Price is the "x" variable, and Demand is the "y" variable. We specify an output range and then "run the regression." We get a very comprehensive output report. Selected output is shown in Table 9.2.

	Coefficients	Standard Error	t Stat	P-value
Intercept	131.60	12.98	10.14	< 0.0001
Price	14.00	3.65	-3.83	0.0050

Table 9.2. Slope and Intercept for Diet Dr. Pepper Data Set

The table shows the slope and intercept values that we learned earlier. The other presented data is discussed next.

9.3.2　Testing the Slope and Intercept

Now that we know the values of the slope and intercept, we need to address the question as to whether or not they are statistically significant. To do this, we first present the linear model relating "x" and "y" for an entire population:

$$Y = \alpha + \beta X \qquad \text{(Eq. 9-3)}$$

Here, the "x" and "y" terms are capitalized to imply data from the entire population. This equation shows "α," which represents the intercept for the population[4], while "β" represents the slope for the population. We need to test the slope and intercept for statistical significance. These hypotheses are as follows:

$$H_0: \; \alpha = 0; \; H_A: \; \alpha \neq 0 \qquad \text{(Eq. 9-4)}$$

$$H_0: \; \beta = 0; \; H_A: \; \beta \neq 0 \qquad \text{(Eq. 9-5)}$$

Eq. 8-4 is a test for the significance of the intercept, while Eq. 8-5 is a test for the significance of the slope. The test for the intercept is not of importance here – the intercept is important in terms of minimizing the sum of squared error value, but for this book, the statistical significance of the intercept is not a matter of concern. What is important, however, is the test for the statistical significance of the slope. In Eq. 8-5, the H_0 states that the slope is equal to zero. This means that as X changes, Y does not change – Y is not sensitive to X. The H_A says that the slope is not equal to zero, meaning that as X changes, Y changes as well – Y is sensitive to X.

These tests for the significance of the slope and intercept are always as presented in these two equations. They are always two-tailed tests. Because of this consistency, we never have to formally state them – they are always the same. This provides Excel, or whatever software is being used to present us the appropriate statistics to interpret. We have to, of course, compare these hypothesized values to the estimated values, which we know to be "a" for the intercept and "b" for the slope. The test statistic for the intercept is as follows:

$$t = \frac{a - \alpha}{se_a} = \frac{a - 0}{se_a} = \frac{a}{se_a} \qquad \text{(Eq. 9-6)}$$

[4] Not to be confused with the level of significance as covered previously. These two entities are independent from each other.

The test statistic for the slope is as follows:

$$t = \frac{b - \beta}{se_b} = \frac{b - 0}{se_b} = \frac{b}{se_b} \qquad \text{(Eq. 9-7)}$$

Because both α and β are hypothesized to be zero, we substitute zero into both equations above, and we end up with the "estimates" of the intercept (a) and slope (b) divided by their standard errors. The end result is the two t-statistics above very closely resemble the t-statistics we used in Chapter 7.

The results of these two-tailed tests are also shown in Table 8.2. When the estimates of the slope and intercept are divided by their standard errors, we have the appropriate t-statistics and p-values. You will notice that the p-value associated with the intercept is < 0.0001. Here, we reject the H_0, and claim the intercept is statistically significant. The t-statistic associated with the slope term is -3.83, with an associated p-value of 0.0050. This tells us that the relationship between Demand and Price is statistically significant – there is a meaningful relationship between price and demand.

9.4 Estimation / Prediction

Let's continue with our Diet Dr. Pepper example and assume that we are satisfied with the belief that Price and Demand have a statistically significant relationship. We can then use the following equation to estimate Demand given some pre-specified or pre-determined Price:

$$\text{Demand} = 131.60 - 14.00(\text{Price}) \qquad \text{(Eq. 9-8)}$$

Given this relationship, however, we need to be careful of the values of Price we use to estimate demand. This model was constructed using a minimum Price of $3.38 and a maximum value of $3.72. Because of this, we can only use this model to estimate Demand for values of price in this interval. If we fail to do this, we are, in essence, "extrapolating," which is a pretentious term for "guessing." As such, we should only estimate for values of "x" that are between x_{min} and x_{max}.

There is one other statistic worth discussing, which is the R^2 value. The value of R^2 tells us the percent of variation in our "y" variable that is explained by our "x" variable. This measure of R^2 is essentially a measure of the model's predictive ability. The R^2 value can be as low as zero, and as high as one. We want our R^2 value to be as high as possible, as that would maximize the percent variation in "y" that is explained by "x." For our example problem, the R^2 value is 0.6473. This value is also included with our Excel output. This means that 64.73% of the variation in Demand is explained by Price. This implies, then, that 35.27% of the variation in Demand has not been explained. As such, when using this model for prediction purposes, we should temper our expectations on the quality of our predictive ability, because much of the variation in demand is explained by entities other than price.

9.5 Conclusions

As stated at the beginning of this chapter, linear regression is the study of relationships among variables. This means that our paramount interest is to see if two variables are related. If they are related – meaning we reject the H_0 regarding a slope of zero – then, and one then, can we pursue the topic of prediction. In short, significance is more important than prediction.

With multiple linear regression – using multiple independent variables ("x" variables), we have the ability to increase our predictive ability via increasing the R^2 value associated with a model.

For now, however, it is most important to understand that simple linear regression is mainly concerned about whether or not variables are related, while multiple linear regression is most concerned about optimizing the predictive ability of our model.

9.6 Exercises

1.   Earlier in this chapter, while talking about the Diet Dr. Pepper example, I mentioned that if we increased the sample size, we would decrease the p-value associated with the slope term. Why is this the case?

2.   Let us revisit the "ExamScores" data set that we used in Chapter 2. This data set has two columns: the "Exam 1" column is the Exam 1 score for a specific student. The "Exam 2" column is the Exam 2 score for the same student. Explain how simple linear regression could be used as a tool to study the student's propensity for success.

3.   Using the "ExamScores" data set, are Exam 1 scores and Exam 2 scores related?

4.   Using the "ExamScores" data set, report the R^2 term with the Exam 1 score as the independent variable and the Exam 2 score as the dependent variable.

5.   Using the "ExamScores" data set, report the R^2 term with the Exam 2 score as the independent variable and the Exam 1 score as the dependent variable.

6.   How do you reconcile your results from the above two questions?

7.   Using the "ExamScores" data set, what score would you expect a student to get on Exam 2 if they got an 83 on Exam 1?

8.   Using the "NewspaperAdvertisements" data set, report on the relationship between Ads/Month and Customers/Month. Is the relationship meaningful?

9.   Using the "NewspaperAdvertisements" data set, estimate customers visiting the store per month when 15 advertisements were made for a specific month. Are you comfortable with this estimate? Why or why not?

10.   Using the "NewspaperAdvertisements" data set, estimate customers visiting the store per month when 23 advertisements were made for a specific month. Are you comfortable with this estimate? Why or why not?

11.   Using the "NewspaperAdvertisements" data set, what is the predictive ability of this model?

12.   Using the "BaseballSalaries2014" data set, report on the relationship between the team payroll and winning percentage. Is the relationship meaningful? Do these results surprise you? Why or why not?

13.   Using the "BaseballSalaries2014" data set, estimate a team's winning percentage with an annual payroll of $150M. Are you comfortable with this estimate? Why or why not?

14.   Using the "BaseballSalaries2014" data set, estimate a team's winning percentage with an annual payroll of $300M. Are you comfortable with this estimate? Why or why not?

15. Using the "BaseballSalaries2014" data set, describe the predictive ability of your model.

16. Look at the two regression plots below. For each plot, the ordinary least squares regression line is fitted through the data. Of the two plots, which one has the higher R^2 value. Justify your response.

10.　Multiple Linear Regression

In our simple linear regression chapter, we explored the relationship between two variables. This chapter had an emphasis on relationships – whether or not the two variables had a statistically significant relationship. We continue our discussion in this chapter, but here, we emphasize predictive ability – finding a model that gives us the highest possible predictive ability. We do this by adding independent variables, which we also refer to as **predictor variables**. The practice of studying such relationships when multiple predictor variables are involved is called **multiple linear regression** or "MLR" for short.

10.1　Improving Predictive Ability

Let us recall our Diet Dr. Pepper example from the simple linear regression chapter. We established a relationship between price and demand for Diet Dr. Pepper. We discovered that the slope term was significant (t = -3.90, p = 0.0045). We also learned that our R^2 term was 0.6553 – 65.53% of the variation in Demand is explained by Price. This means that 34.47% (1 - 0.6553) of the variation in Demand is explained by something other than Price. If we are interested in estimating or predicting Demand, it seems that we'd like more predictive ability.

10.1.1　Adding More Variables

More predictive ability can be obtained if we add more predictor (independent) variables to our model. This can be done quite easily in Excel – when we are asked for the "X" variables, we simply "paint" all of the independent variables.[5]

Let us continue our Diet Dr. Pepper example from the Simple Linear Regression chapter. This time, however, we will add a predictor variable "Advertising," which represents the number of signs advertising the Diet Dr. Pepper. The advertising is done in the proximity of the store. The new data set, then, is as follows:

---

[5] To "paint" the necessary predictor variables, they must be in adjacent columns. Otherwise, Excel cannot process them. Columns of predictor variables in non-adjacent columns will not work in Excel.

Price	3.38	3.42	3.48	3.52	3.55	3.55	3.61	3.61	3.67	3.72
Adv.	28	30	28	26	26	28	26	26	26	27
Dem.	83	86	83	81	81	83	81	81	80	80

Table 10.1. Price and Advertising vs. Demand Data for Diet Dr. Pepper

We then ask Excel to perform the linear regression. This time, however, we make certain that both Price and Advertising are treated as "x" variables.

10.1.2 F-Statistic and Regression Output

Prior to discussing the regression output of the example problem, it is appropriate for us to address the hypothesis testing associated with multiple linear regression. When examining the output, the first thing one should consider is the general set of hypotheses that accompany such analyses. The null and alternative hypotheses are as follows:

H_0: The independent variables are not related to
the dependent variable   (Eq. 10-1)
H_A: The independent variables are related to the
dependent variable

The hypotheses stated above are always the case. As such, there is no need to explicitly define them.

To determine whether or not to reject the H_0, we examine the following statistic, which we refer to as the "F-statistic."

$$F = \frac{Explained\ Variation}{Unexplained\ Variation}$$ (Eq. 10-2)

This statistic should not look entirely unfamiliar. We saw something very similar when we discussed the Analysis of Variance. If this ratio is high (the associated p-value being less than some threshold value, such as 0.05), we reject the H_0 and claim that there is a meaningful relationship between the independent and dependent variables.[6]

For our example problem, our F-statistic is 46.19, with an associated p-

---

[6] In truth, the significance of the F-statistic in multiple linear regression almost always shows significance, because we are trying to optimize the predictive ability, which strongly implies a significant relationship between the "x" and "y" variables already exists.

value of < 0.0001. Therefore, both Price and Advertising have a meaningful relationship with Demand.

The next order of business is to determine whether or not our predictor variables are statistically significant. Selected regression output is shown in Table 10.2.

	Coefficients	Standard Error	t Stat	P-value
Intercept	79.27	11.87	6.68	0.0003
Price	-6.36	2.30	-2.77	0.0278
Advertisement	0.93	0.18	5.22	0.0012

Table 10.2. Intercept and Slopes for MLR Diet Dr. Pepper Problem

Here we see that the intercept and both slope terms are statistically significant – all p-values are very small. You will also notice that the values of the intercept and the Price slope have changed from the simple linear regression ("SLR") problem. This should not be a surprise, because with the addition of the new term (Advertisement) all other terms will have new values in the pursuit of minimizing the sum of squared errors term.

Now that we can take comfort in that we have a meaningful relationship between Demand and the predictor variables of Price and Advertisements, we can turn our attention to prediction. Excel tells us that our R^2 value is 0.9296. This means that 92.96% of the variation in Demand is explained by both Price and Advertisements. This is a great improvement over the R^2 value from our earlier model, where Price was the only predictor variable for Demand. In general, adding predictor variables to a linear regression will result in an increase in R^2. As such, adding variables to a model improves our predictive ability.

We can now predict Demand by using the predictors of Price and Advertisements via the following equation:

$$\text{Demand} = 79.27 - (6.36)(\text{Price}) + (0.93)(\text{Advertisements})$$

(Eq. 10-3)

We must, however, bear in mind that when predicting; make sure we use values of the predictor variables that are in range of the values from our data set. Otherwise, we are extrapolating, which can provide unreliable results.

10.2   Multicollinearity

Let us consider another example, where I am interested in estimating GMAT Score using the predictor variables of undergraduate GPA and Hours Studying for the GMAT exam. This sounds like a reasonable experiment. It seems reasonable to expect that as both undergraduate GPA and Hours Studying increase, so would the associated GMAT score.

To further investigate this, the data set "GMATExample" has been provided. When performing a multiple linear regression where GMAT score is the dependent (response variable), and GPA and Hours Studying are the predictor variables, we have an F-statistic of 824.93, with an associated p-value < 0.0001. We also have an R^2 value of 0.6238. So far, so good.

When we look at the statistical significance of the individual predictor variables, however, we have the following:

	Coefficients	Standard Error	t Stat	P-value
Intercept	-255.47	41.80	-6.11	< 0.0001
GPA	205.93	44.25	4.65	< 0.0001
Hours Studying	2.96	2.35	1.26	0.2091

Table 10.3. Predictor Variables for GMAT Example

When looking at the table above, a problem becomes evident. The slope term for Hours Studying doesn't show statistical significance. We are being told that there is no relationship between Hours Studying and GMAT score. This doesn't make sense. Upon further investigation, a simple linear regression is performed between GMAT score and Hours studying – GPA is excluded from this analysis. This regression reveals that Hours Studying is in fact related to GMAT score (t = 39.94, p < 0.0001).

In summary, multiple linear regression tells us that Hours Studying is not related to GMAT score, while simple linear regression tells us that Hours Studying is related to GMAT score. These conflicting results are a consequence of **multicollinearity** – a strong correlation between predictor variables. While multicollinearity does not have any impact of our ability for prediction, it greatly impedes our ability to interpret individual predictor variables.

10.2.1 Correlation

When we define multicollinearity above, we state that it is the presence of a strong correlation of predictor variables. Now **correlation** must be defined. Correlation is a degree of relationship between variables. That definition sounds eerily familiar – simple linear regression explores relationships between variables. The difference between correlation and simple linear regression is that simple linear regression explains the relationship between slope and intercept, along with the results of associated hypothesis tests, while correlation provides a single standardized statistic describing the relationship between the two variables of interest.

This single standardized statistic used to measure correlation is called the correlation coefficient, ρ. This value of ρ is always in the interval ($-1 \leq \rho \leq 1$). This value of ρ, intended to measure the correlation between "x" and "y," is determined as follows:

$$\rho = \frac{\sum_{i=1}^{n}(x_i - \bar{x})(y_i - \bar{y})}{\sqrt{\sum_{i=1}^{n}(x_i - \bar{x})^2/(n-1)}\sqrt{\sum_{i=1}^{n}(y_i - \bar{y})^2/(n-1)}} \qquad \text{(Eq. 10-4)}$$

Fortunately, this value is calculated for us using the "=correl($range1, range2$)" function in Excel. Of greater value, however, is the use of the correlation matrix tool available in the Data Analysis Tools. The correlation matrix tool will provide an entire matrix of pairwise correlations between all variables selected. Using this tool for the data in our problem, we have the following:

	GMAT Score	GPA	Hours Studying
GMAT Score	1		
GPA	0.7894	1	
Hours Studying	0.7846	0.9894	1

Table 10.4. Correlation Matrix for GMAT Score Example Problem

10.2.2 Remediation

If we take a close look at our correlation matrix above, we see that we have also included the response variable of GMAT Score. This will be discussed further momentarily. For now, you should take notice of the correlation of 0.9894 – the standardized relationship between the two predictor variables, GPA and hours studying. This means that Hours Studying and GPA are essentially telling us the same thing. Because of this, we have multicollinearity, and when two predictors are highly correlated, our regression output can be counterintuitive. Such is the case here – our multiple regression output tells us that Hours Studying *is not* meaningful, when simple regression tells us Hours Studying *is* meaningful.

What do we do when we get conflicting results like this? There are many opinions on this matter, but I strongly prefer the most **parsimonious** approach. I prefer to remove one of the correlated variables, and let it be explained by the remaining variable. In this situation, it makes the most sense to remove Hours Studying and let it be explained by GPA, because its correlation with GMAT score (the response variable) is less than GPA's correlation with GMAT score (0.7846 < 0.7894).

Because we have removed Hours Studying and let it be explained by GPA, our model reduces to GMAT score as the dependent variable, and with only GPA as our independent variable.

10.3   Parsimony

With having only one predictor variable now, we once again perform a linear regression without Hours Studying as a predictor variable. The results are as follows:

	Coefficients	Std. Error	t Stat	P-value
Intercept	-302.03	19.36	-15.60	< 0.0001
GPA	260.96	6.43	40.59	< 0.0001

Table 10.5. GMAT Score as a Function of GPA Only

Of course, the lone slope of GPA is highly significant (t = 40.59, p < 0.0001). Most importantly, however, is the R^2 value, which is 0.6232 – 62.32% of the variation in GMAT score is explained by GPA. Comparing that to the multiple regression model, where GMAT score is explained by GPA and Hours studying, we have an R^2 of 0.6238. In other words, by removing Hours Studying from our model, we only lose 0.0006 from our R^2 term. A meaningless loss.

This simple example best illustrates the most important aspect of multiple regression, which is **parsimony**. The word "parsimony" is not used much anymore, but it generally implies thrift.[7] In the context of model-fitting, parsimony is intended to suggest the use of as few variables as possible to get the most predictive model. In our present situation, the model with one predictor variable is far superior to the one with two predictor variables because we get the same predictive power with one less term to "worry" about and/or discuss.

10.4   Conclusions

Simple Linear Regression is a tool to explore whether or not relationships exist between variables. With only a single predictor variable, we would be naïve to assume Simple Linear Regression as a good predictive tool. This is where Multiple Linear Regression comes in. Multiple Linear Regression builds on relationships (uncovered by Simple Linear Regression) and attempts to optimize the predictive fit by adding variables. Those variables, however, should be chosen wisely. When the appropriate variables are added, our R^2 term approaches a value of 1.00, resulting in a good predictive model.

If we choose too many predictor variables, we can still have a good predictive model, but we lose our ability to explain our model in a concise manner. We should always attempt to maximize the R^2 term with as few predictor variables as possible.

10.5   Exercises

1. A company that delivers equipment is attempting to understand what determines annual maintenance cost for their fleet of their nine trucks. A data set named "TruckMaintainence" is to be used, where data is given for each truck including the annual maintenance cost for each truck, the number of miles on the truck, and the age of the truck in years. Using $\alpha = 0.05$, please address the following:

---

[7] Charles Dickens often used the word "parsimony" in his work. In the Dickensian context, it implies "thrift" – not spending more money than needed. In our work here, it is important not to use more words and/or variables than needed.

    a. Yes or No: is there an overall relationship between the annual maintenance cost of the truck with the predictor variables of mileage of the truck and the age of the truck.

    b. Justify your response above.

    c. Is the current parsimonious? Why or why not?

    d. What is the most parsimonious model? Justify your response.

2. The data set named "CollegeProbability" contains three variables of data. These variables are "College Prob," "Class Size," and "SAT Score." Definitions of these variables are as follows:

College Prob: this is the probability that the student in question will attend college.

Class Size: this is the number of students from the class in which the student in question comes.

SAT Score: this is the SAT score that the student in question earned.

For example, the very first data point tells us that the student in question has a 63.52% chance of attending college. This particular student came from a class size of 21, and earned a score of 1232 on the SAT test.

Your job for this problem is to find the most parsimonious model that explains the probability of attending college. When finding this model, explain the steps you have taken **without** use of Excel terminology.

3. We are interested in determining the driving forces behind mutual fund performance. The attached data set, called "MutualFundPerformance" contains annual return data (in %) for several mutual funds. For each fund, experience (in years) of the mutual fund's manager is provided, along with the fund manager's salary (in $1,000s). The fund type is also provided, which is either a stock fund or bond fund. Using this data, please address the following questions:

    a. Do the experience of the fund manager, the salary of the fund manager, and the fund type have an aggregate relationship with the mutual fund's performance?

    b. Explain the model you used in part "a" above.

    c. Using the model constructed in part "a" above, estimate the fund's return for a bond fund with a fund manager earning a salary of $200,000/year and 12 years experience?

    d.   Is multicollinearity a problem? Why or why not?

    e.   What is the most parsimonious model that should be used to explain the mutual fund's annual return? Justify your response.

4. I have a data set ("MyStockData") which details daily stock prices of MyStock – a stock that I own. I am trying to use three other stocks to analyze and predict the price of MyStock. Using the attached information, along with a value of α = 0.01, please address the following questions:

    a.   Yes or No: do Stocks A, B and C have an aggregate relationship with MyStock?

    b.   Support your above response.

    c.   Yes or No: Is multicollinearity a problem?

    d.   Support your above response.

    e.   What is the most parsimonious model? Explain your reasoning.

    f.   If Stocks A, B and C are priced at $35, $17, $86 respectively, what would expect the price of MyStock to be, when using the most parsimonious model?

5. A beer distributor needs to understand the relationship between the response variable of delivery time and the two predictor variables of distance to travel and the number of cases to deliver. This data is provided ("BeerDistributionTime"). Using this data, please answer the following questions:

    a.   Is there an aggregate relationship between delivery time and the two predictor variables of distance to travel and cases to deliver?

    b.   Justify your above answer.

    c.   Is multicollinearity a problem? Why or why not?

    d.   What is the most parsimonious model? Explain your reasoning.

6. A junior golf tournament was held in Walnut Creek, California. There were 500 participants – all of them boys. These participants ranged in age from as young as 13 to as old as 18. For each participant, their 18-hole score was recorded, along with their handicap (a basic measure of the golfer's skill), age, and the number of hours per week

that the golfer of interest practices.   This data is included ("JuniorGolfTournament"). Using this information, please address the following:

    a.   Do age, handicap and hours/week of practice time have an aggregate relationship with the tournament score? Why or why not?

    b. Which predictor variable has the strongest relationship with score? Explain your rationale.

    c. Is multicollinearity present? Why or why not.

    d. Using the most parsimonious model, estimate the score of a 14-year-old with a handicap of 15 who practices 19 hours/week.

11. Analysis of Variance (ANOVA)

It is often important for us to determine whether or not means from different populations are similar. In fact, we did this exact thing in the hypothesis testing chapter. Unfortunately, the tools provided in that chapter restrict us to exploring similarity in means when only two populations are involved. This chapter provides the tools to explore similarity in means from two or more populations.

When determining whether or not populations differ in terms of mean values, it is helpful to define a few new terms. A **factor** is categorical variable, also known as a **treatment**. It can be thought of as a data type. When considering the hypothetical example of determining whether or not defects per million units produced are the same across each shift, the shift can be thought of as a factor. This factor, for this particular example, has three unique **levels**: first, second and third shifts. Using this terminology, we can relate the measured value to the factor. For instance, we can ask the same question in mathematical form as follows:

Defects / Million Units Produced = f(Shift)

This question is asking whether or not defects per million units produced is related to the shift. If defects are related to shift, we can conclude that shift does have an effect on defects. Otherwise, we must conclude that shift does not have an effect on shift.

11.1 Variation and the F-Distribution

To determine whether or not means are the same across multiple populations (there are a populations), we first need to establish the appropriate hypotheses. They are as follows:

$$H_0: \ \mu_1 = \mu_2 = \mu_3 \ldots = \ldots \mu_a \qquad \text{(Eq. 11-1)}$$
$$H_A: \text{ not all means are equal}$$

The reason this tool is called Analysis of Variance ("ANOVA" for short) is because at the heart of our analysis, we are comparing two variations. The F-statistic does this via a ratio of two measures of variation. Before presenting this statistic, we need to define a few terms.

Term	Definition
a	number of groups, or populations
n_i	sample size of group i (i = 1, 2, ..., a)
$\bar{x}_i$	sample mean of group i
s_i	sample standard deviation of group i
x_{it}	the ith observation of group t
$\bar{\bar{x}}$	mean of all sample data

Table 11.1. Terms Used for ANOVA

The values in Table 11.1 are used to determine the F-statistic, which is the ratio of two variation measures. In its most general form, the F-statistic looks like this:

$$F = \frac{Between\ Group\ Variation}{Within\ Group\ Variation} \qquad \text{(Eq. 11-2)}$$

What this statistic tells us is that F measures how much "distance" there is between groups compared to how much variation each group has on its own. If this ratio is large, we can claim that group means are in fact statistically different (reject H_0). Otherwise, we cannot claim a significant difference between groups (fail to reject H_0). In more specific terms, our F-statistic looks like this:

$$F = \frac{\sum_{i=1}^{a} n_i(\bar{x}_i - \bar{\bar{x}})^2/(a-1)}{\sum_{i=1}^{a}\sum_{t=1}^{n_i}(x_{it} - \bar{x}_i)^2/\sum_{i=1}^{a}(n_i-1)} \qquad \text{(Eq. 11-3)}$$

There is no doubt that the formula above is complicated, and inappropriate for business students to pursue. Fortunately, Microsoft Excel and other software packages calculate this value for us. More on this shortly.

It is appropriate to note that like for other hypothesis tests, a p-value accompanies the F-statistic, and like with other p-values we've pursued, a smaller p-value implies we should reject the H_0.

As an example of the F-statistic and how it determines significant differences in means between groups, we turn to a simple ANOVA example, where there are two groups. Specifically, an issue I deal with when teaching statistics to my MBA students. On Monday evening, I give an exam to my Working Professional students in Charlotte. On Tuesday evening, I give the same exam to my Working Professional students in Winston-Salem. After grading the exams, I am always interested in seeing whether or not there is a difference in performance between the two classes – I want both classes to do well, and sometimes I fear that one group is doing better (or worse) than the other. ANOVA is the ideal tool to help me address this question. These examples are presented in the context of the F-statistic, and its associated p-value.

Consider a scenario where the exam score for the Charlotte class is about 86, and the average exam score for the Winston-Salem class is about 85. The standard deviation for both classes is about 5.5. The F-statistic for this scenario is 1.52 (and an associated p-value of 0.7971), with a between group variation of 39.20, and a within group variation of 25.8. Clearly, there is no significant difference between the groups. Figure 11-1 supports this via a combined histogram for the two classes.

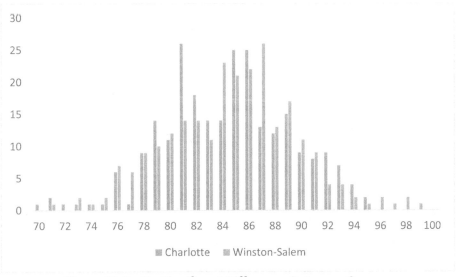

Figure 11.1. No Significant Difference Between Groups.

From a graphical standpoint, Figure 11.1 shows no separation between the two groups. As such, we are unable to claim any differences between the groups.

Now we consider a scenario where the means of the two groups are the same as they were before, but this time, the sample standard deviations are about 4 for each group. This results in an F-statistic of 2.80, with a between group variation of 45.00 and a within group variation of 16.05. The F-statistic has an associated p-value of about 0.0947. Figure 11-2 shows the combined histogram of this scenario.

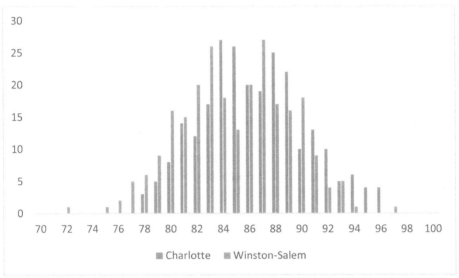

Figure 11-2. Some Significant Difference Between Groups

Here, we may notice that there is some evidence that the Charlotte class has done slightly better than the Winston-Salem class, because there is more "blue" to the right, and more "red" to the left. Nevertheless, our evidence is less than compelling.

As a final example, let us consider once again that Charlotte's average is about 86, while the Winston-Salem average is about 85. This time, however, the standard deviation for both classes is about 1. This gives us an F-statistic of 100.66 (and an associated p-value of < 0.0001), a between group variation of 106.72 and a within group variation of 1.06. Figure 11-3 shows us the results via a combined histogram.

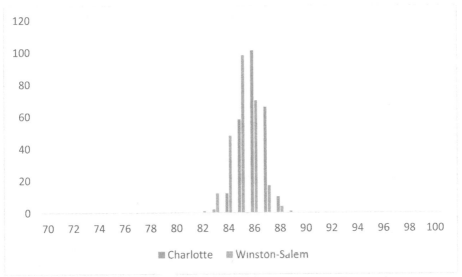

Figure 11.3. Significant Difference Between Groups.

Figure 11.3 shows that there is a definite difference in groups.

The point in showing these three scenarios is to emphasize how the F-statistic controls our decision as to whether or not to reject H_0. In each of these scenarios, the difference in means is about 1 point, implying that the between group variation is essentially the same. But as we proceed through the example, our within group variation decreases, thereby increasing the F-statistic, making us more likely to reject H_0. Difference in means can be small, but if there is consistency within each group, we can still claim significant differences between groups. This is what the F-statistic tells us.

11.2   Testing Equality of Means from Multiple Populations

Fortunately, we do not have to construct H_0 and H_A for ANOVA tests. The reason for this is because the test is the same way every time. H_0 states that all means are equal, while H_A states that not all means are equal. This never changes. As such, software packages always compute the means and standard deviations for each group, and them compute the F-statistic and report the associated p-value.

As an example, consider the Excel data set "ShiftDefectData." For this data set, there is a column for each of three shifts of a factory. Each data value shows the number of defects per million units for the appropriate shift. We are interested in knowing if defects per million are the same for each shift. This is very straightforward in Microsoft Excel. We need to have an Excel data set with a unique column for each unique population – in this case, each population is a shift. We use the Data Analysis tools and select "ANOVA: Single Factor." From there, we select the data we wish to use for analysis. Again, each column represents a unique population. We indicate whether or not our data set has column headings, we input our level of significance (α = 0.05) is the default. We then select our desired output range then select OK. We are given the ANOVA output, which is summarized in Table 11-2.

Groups	Count	Sum	Average	Variance
Shift 1	62	3033	48.92	219.42
Shift 2	62	2733	44.08	174.08
Shift 3	62	2913	46.98	258.80

Variation Source	SS	df	MS	F	P-val
Between Groups	735.48	2	367.74	1.69	0.1871
Within Groups	39790	183	217.43		
Total	40526	185			

Table 11-2. ANOVA Output for Defects by Shift Problem

The first part of Figure 11-2 shows the descriptive statistics for each of the three shifts. The average number of defects per shift is of greatest interest to us. You will notice that the defects per million for the three shifts ranges from around 44 to about 49. The ANOVA table below shows the F-statistic (F = 1.69) and its associated p-value. You will see that the p-value is high (0.1871), which prevents us from saying the defects per million units made are essentially the same for each shift. Because of this, I am reluctant to present a combined histogram of defects/million for each shift, as we'd be unable to show any distinction between the histograms. For this problem, we can conclude that shift *does not* have an effect on defects. Incidentally, the remainder of the ANOVA table simply shows the derivation of the F-statistic.

As another example, let us look at the useful life of tools coated with three different metals: nickel, phosphorus and zinc. We wish to study the useful tool life for each group of tools.

Figure 11-4. Useful Tool Life by Metal Treatment

From the combined histogram in Figure 11.4, it appears that phosphorus gives us the longest tool life, followed by zinc, with nickel providing us with the shortest tool life. However, we cannot make this statement in any official capacity until we perform the appropriate ANOVA test. Using Excel in a similar fashion to the last example, we have the following ANOVA output, as shown in Table 11.3.

Groups	Count	Sum	Average	Variance
Phosphorus	890	71090	79.88	10.30
Zinc	878	57864	65.90	16.38
Nickel	872	48867	56.04	33.30

Variation Source	SS	df	MS	F	P-val
Between Groups	253026	2	126513	6352.38	0[8]
Within Groups	52518	2637	20		
Total	305544	2639			

Table 11.3. ANOVA Output for Tool Life by Metal Treatment Problem

As one can see from Figures 11.4 and Table 11.3, there is strong evidence for us to claim that the three metal treatments do not result in similar useful tool lives, with F = 6352.38 and a corresponding p-value < 0.0001. Despite the p-value showing "0" above, we can never claim a p-value equal to 0, so we say that is it < 0.0001. The reason for this is that we are using sample data from a larger population, and the p-value will always have value in excess of 0. For this problem, we can conclude that the metal treatment *does have* an effect on tool life.

11.3   Multiple Factor Analysis of Variance

Thus far, we have pursued ANOVA via a single factor only. There are situations where multiple factors might also be considered. When two or more factors are studied, we have a multiple factor scenario.

11.3.1 Interaction of Factors

What if we were interested in studying whether or not both the gender of the salesperson and the personality type of the salesperson has an effect on car sales. We could pose this question mathematically:

Car Sales = f(Gender of Salesperson, Personality Type of Salesperson)

This question has two factors (Gender and Personality Type), where Gender has two levels (Male and Female), and Personality Type has two levels (Type

---

[8] Excel displays the p-value here as "0," but it should be "< 0.0001." Excel does this when confronted with p-values less than 10^{-256}.

A and Type B). We can pursue these types of questions via Multiple Factor ANOVA. Unfortunately, adding factors to ANOVA problems complicates the problem to a very large degree. Fortunately, Excel can assist with two-factor ANOVA. In order to do this, we have to organize our spreadsheet in a way such that Excel understands that we are dealing with a two-factor scenario. One of the factors has to be expressed in columns, as was the case with Single-Factor ANOVA. The second factor, however, must occupy a specific number of rows. Figure 11.4 displays a very simplified example of data prepared for Two Factor Analysis.

	Factor 1 (Level A)	Factor 1 (Level B)
Factor 2 (Level A)	Observation 1 Observation 2 Observation 3, etc.	Observation 1 Observation 2 Observation 3, etc.
Factor 2 (Level B)	Observation 1 Observation 2 Observation 3, etc.	Observation 1 Observation 2 Observation 3, etc.

Figure 11.4. Excel Layout for Two-Factor ANOVA

One will notice that this problem has four unique factor-level combinations. The factor level combinations will always be the product of the number of levels for each factor. The above example also has three observations for each factor level combination. For Excel to perform Two Factor ANOVA properly, the number of observations for each factor-level combination must be the same.[9]

To continue our example, we will use the "GenderPersonalityType.xlsx" worksheet. In order to perform our analysis, we need to use the Data Analysis Tools. Here we select "ANOVA: Two Factor with Replication." We are then asked to specify the input range. Here, enter the entire data set, including row and column headings. Next, we asked to input the number of rows per sample. Here you enter the number of observations for each unique factor level combination, which is 14 for this example. Next, we are asked to enter the pre-specified value of α. To finish, we enter the location for our output

---

[9] Other statistical software packages, such as "R" and "JMP" permit a varying number of observations for each factor level combination.

report. This is illustrated in Figure 11.5.

Figure 11.5. Excel for Two Factor ANOVA

Next, we interpret the output report. One will see tables detailing descriptive statistics for each factor level combination. One will also see three F-statistics – these inform us of the statistical significance of the factors. We see that the "Sample" factor has an F-statistic of 0.68 (p = 0.4143). The "Sample" factor is the factor that is row-oriented. Here, that implies the Personality Type factor. We see that it is not statistically meaningful. In other words, the Personality Type of the sales representative has no relationship with car sales.

We also see an F-statistic of 8.49 (p = 0.0053) for the "Column" factor. This implies the column-oriented factor, which is Gender of the salesperson in our example. We can conclude, then Gender does in fact have a relationship with car sales. Specifically, Males outsell Females – this is from the inspection of the means table.

Next we see that the term called "Interaction" has an F-statistic of 405.25 (p < 0.0001). The interaction term details the effect of both factors simultaneously. Figure 11.6 details the interaction between factors via a plot of means for each factor level combination. The blue line shows the Type A personality, while the orange line shows the Type B personality. Male and Female factor levels are shown on the horizontal axis, while car sales are shown via the vertical axis.

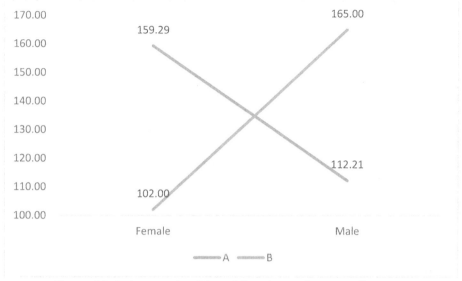

Figure 11.6. Interaction Plot of Gender and Personality Type

From inspection of this chart, we can see that the Type A personality works better for Females, while the Type B personality works best for Males. In other words, Personality Type and Gender are not consistent with each other. This meaningful interaction of factors is best described via Figure 11.6, where the "lines" for a factor are not parallel. Hence, there is a meaningful "relationship" between the factors. If these lines were parallel, we could claim no meaningful interaction. Here, the interaction is very much present.

11.3.2 Non Interaction of Factors

Consider a scenario where we would like to analyze chess ratings according to two factors: age group of the player, and continent of the player. For this example, we have three age groups of Youth, Adult and Senior, and two Continents: American and European. A data set called "ChessScores.xlsx" details this. To perform a two-factor ANOVA in Excel, we choose Data|Data Analysis | ANOVA: Two Factor with Replication. We select the entire data set for the input, we enter 10 rows per sample (because each factor combination has 10 observations), we enter $\alpha = 0.05$, and we select the location for the output report.

From inspection of the output, we see that the Age Group is a statistically meaningful factor (F = 432.75, p < 0.0001). Excel calls this the "Sample" factor, as it is row-oriented. Specifically, Adults have the highest ratings, followed by the Seniors.

Additionally, the Nationality factor is also statistically significant (F = 16.86, p = 0.0001). Excel calls this the "Column" factor, as it is column-oriented. Specifically, the European players have higher ratings as compared to Americans.

The last statistic interpreted is the interaction between Age Group and Nationality. This term is not statistically meaningful (F = 1.15, p = 0.3240). In other words, there is no interaction (relationship) between Nationality and Age Group. This is confirmed in Figure 11.7 – the lines are essentially parallel, unlike what we see in Figure 11.6.

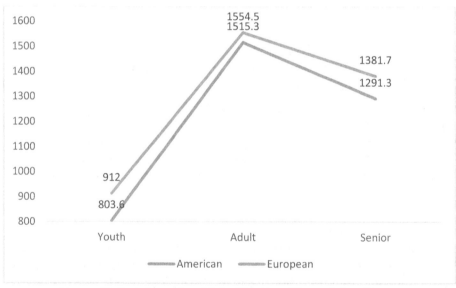

Figure 11.7. Interaction Plot of Nationality and Age Group

It should be noted that the interaction plot is indifferent to the rows and columns. Figure 11.8 shows the same plot as above, but in transposed fashion – the rows and columns have been swapped.

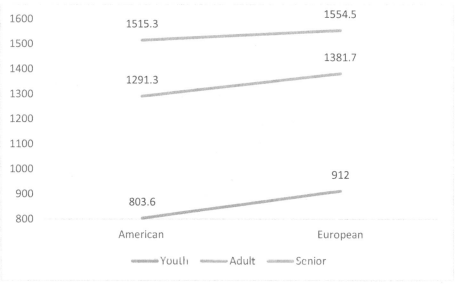

Figure 11.8. Interaction Plot of Age Group and Nationality

Figure 11.8 essentially shows the same result as does Figure 11.7. All the lines are parallel, suggesting the lack of factor interaction. Again, lines that are not parallel suggest a factor interaction.

11.4   Conclusions

ANOVA determines whether or not some factor has an effect on the value of some other variable. This factor can be considered a categorical variable – a variable we cannot precisely measure numerically. Certainly we can assign a number to a shift, but this is only a relative to other shifts. We cannot measure specific metal treatments, gender of a salesperson or a specific day of the week. Nevertheless, we are exploring a possible relationship between a categorical variable and a numerical variable. When we get to the chapter on Simple Linear Regression, our categorical variable will be replaced with a numerical variable. Because of this, there is a strong relationship between Single-Factor ANOVA and Simple Linear Regression. Chapter 9 will pursue this further.

11.5   Exercises

1. I am interested in pursuing the relationship between temperature and the time of day. What is the categorical variable, and what is the numerical variable? How many levels does the categorical variable have?

2. Use the "GenderSalesData" file for this problem. At the $\alpha = 0.05$ level, does Gender have an effect on sales volume? Report the mean sales for each Gender and justify your response accordingly.

3. Use the "GenderSalesData" file for this problem. At the $\alpha = 0.07$ level, does Day of the week have an effect on sales volume? Report the mean sales for each Day and justify your response accordingly.

4. Use the "ServerComplaints" data file for this problem. At the $\alpha = 0.03$ level, does server have an effect on the percent of restaurant customers who complain about the service? Report the mean complaint percentage for each server and justify your response accordingly.

5. Use the "ExamDay" data file for this problem. Professor Fraud teaches statistics on Monday, Wednesday and Friday. When he gives his students an exam, it will be on one of these days. The data set shows randomly selected exam scores for students taking exams on these days. At the $\alpha = 0.05$ level, does the day of the exam have an effect on the exam score? Present the means for the exam days, and use this to justify your result.

6. Use the "WhisperingPines" data set for this question. Arnold, Jack and Tiger are reputable golfers, and Whispering Pines is a famous golf course, with a rich history. There are four Par 5s on the golf course. On a par 5, a professional golfer is expected to get their ball on the green in three shots. However, the best golfers try to get their ball on the green in two shots, so as to increase their probability for a good score. If a golfer gets their ball on the green of a par 5 in two shots, they have been successful at this challenge. The data set includes randomly-selected success rates for Arnold, Jack and Tiger for some of their rounds of golf played at par 5 holes at the Whispering Pines golf course. Using $\alpha = 0.03$, are the success rates unique for the three golfers?

7. As a follow-up to the previous question, is Tiger's success rate unique from that of the other two golfers? Again, use $\alpha = 0.03$.

8. For this question, use the "HousePricesFourCities" data set. There are four cities involved here: Indianapolis, Boston, Rochester and San Diego. For each city, randomly-selected real-estate transaction prices have been shown. At the $\alpha = 0.01$ level, can we say that the city has an effect on the transaction price?

9. Using the same data set as above, and $\alpha = 0.01$, can we claim a difference in transaction price between San Diego and Boston?

10. The data set "IndustrialProcess.xlsx" details the material yield from an industrial process where the items manufactured were exposed to varying Temperatures and varying Pressures. Use this data to determine whether or not the factors of Temperature and/or Pressure have a meaningful relationship with the process yield. What about the interaction of Temperature and Pressure? Use $\alpha = 0.05$.

11. The data set "GolfClubs.xlsx" details the driving distance of three different golf clubs: a traditional driver, a titanium driver with a metal shaft, and a titanium driver with a graphite shaft. Each club was used to hit 15 shots. Additionally, three players of varying skill (Lion, Leopard and Panther) were each used to fifteen shots with each club. Using $\alpha = 0.05$, does the driver have a relationship with distance? Does the golfer have a relationship with drive length? Is there an interaction between the player and the club?

12. Section A meets at 11AM on Monday and Wednesday, while Section B meets at 8AM on Tuesday and Thursday. They take the same exam. Emma grades half of the exams from Section A, and half the exams from Section B. Similarly, Susie grades the other half the exams from Section A, and the other half of the Exams from Section B. The grades of this study are included via the "EmmaAndSusie" worksheet. Using $\alpha = 0.05$, explore he significance of all possible factors. Is the result of the grader's (Emma or Susie) significance good news? Why or why not?

12.　Chi-Square Testing

In our study of statistics, there are often times when we are given a distribution of data and we need to "tell the world" the type of data distribution we have. One way to do this is by inspection. For example, if our histogram shows a peak in the middle of the data, the histogram is symmetric, and low frequencies of outcomes lie in the tails, a normal distribution is a good guess. Unfortunately, it is not always that easy.

Because of these inherent difficulties, we sometimes need to perform a formal test to determine if a given (observed) data distribution fits that of a theoretical (expected) data distribution. In order to do this, we perform a chi-square test.

In this chapter, we will cover two types of chi-square tests. The first is called a "goodness of fit" test to see if a given data distribution matches that of an expected distribution. The second type of test is called a "test of independence," where we determine if the variables associated with a marginal probability table are independent of each other.

12.1　The Chi-Square Test

The formal test to determine if an observed distribution matches a theoretical data distribution is a chi-square test. The appropriate hypotheses are as follows:

H_0: the given distribution fits the expected distribution　　(Eq. 12-1)
H_A: the given distribution does not fit the expected distribution

As is the case with ANOVA, these hypotheses are always the case, and the need to formally state these hypotheses is not as necessary as it is for the tests we performed in the hypothesis testing chapter.

The chi-square distribution is the tool we use to address the hypotheses presented above. This distribution formally tests whether or not there is equality in two sets of outcomes. Of course, for our purposes, one set of outcomes is the observed distribution and the other set of outcomes is the expected distribution. With this stated, assuming we have n possible outcomes, we compare the observed frequencies (f_o) with the expected frequencies, and derive our chi-square test-statistic as follows:

$$\chi^2 = \sum_{i=1}^{n} \left(\frac{\left(f_{o(i)} - f_{e(i)}\right)^2}{fe_{(i)}} \right) \qquad \text{(Eq. 12-2)}$$

This statistic takes the squared difference between the observed and expected frequencies for each outcome and then divides by the expected frequency for standardization purposes. The summation accounts for all possible outcomes. If this value exceeds some critical value, we reject H_0 and claim a difference between observed and expected distributions. Table 12-1 shows the critical value and p-values associated with a chi-square test for a level of significance = α and n possible outcomes.

Function	Definition
chiinv(α, n-1)	critical value of a chi-square test
chidist(χ^2, n-1)	p-value of a chi-square test

Table 12-1. Excel Functions for Chi-Square Test

12.2 Goodness of Fit Test

The simplest type of chi-square test is to see whether or not a given set of observed data fits an expected distribution, which, as we stated earlier, is called a "goodness of fit" test.

A good example of this is to roll a single die 100 times and study the frequency of the six possible outcomes. Given that we expect each outcome to occur with a 1/6 probability, each outcome over 100 trials will be 100/6, which is 16.66. Table 12-2 shows the observed frequencies, compared to the expected frequencies when 100 rolls were simulated. The table also shows the by-outcome detail of the chi-square statistic shown in Eq. 12-2.

Outcome	1	2	3	4	5	6
Observed	21	13	9	21	17	19
Expected	16.67	16.67	16.67	16.67	16.67	16.67
$(f_o-f_e)^2/f_e$	1.13	0.81	3.53	1.13	0.01	0.33

Table 12-2. Chi-Square Test for Single Die Roll

When we sum the bottom row of this table, we have a χ^2 statistic of 6.92. Using a $\alpha = 0.05$ level of significance, we have a critical value of 11.07. Because our χ^2 test statistic of 6.92 does not exceed our critical value of 11.07, we cannot reject the H_0. As such, we conclude the expected distribution is the same as the given distribution, with a p-value of 0.2267. In layman's terms, we can claim the single die "is fair." Figure 12-1 below shows the results via a histogram – notice the small difference in the height of each bar.

Figure 12-1. Histogram of Die Roll

We can also test a data set of observed data to see if they follow a normal distribution. We learned that a normal distribution is a continuous distribution (one with infinite possible outcomes), which doesn't coordinate well with the discrete nature of chi-square testing. Nevertheless, we can use the "norm.dist" function in Excel to transform the continuous nature of a normal distribution to one with a discrete nature. The "norm.dist" function takes on the following form:

$$f(x_i) = \text{norm.dist}(\mu,\ \sigma,\ x_i,\ \text{false}) \qquad \text{(Eq. 12-3)}$$

This function returns the normal density function associated with the given arguments: μ is the hypothesized population mean; σ is the standard deviation of the normal distribution; x_i is a specific outcome, and "false" request the density function value associated with these arguments, as opposed to the cumulative density function. We can convert this density function to a probability – specifically the probability of outcome i occurring as follows:

$$P(x_i) = \frac{norm.\,dist(\mu, \sigma, x_i, false)}{\sum_{i=1}^{n} norm.\,dist(\mu, \sigma, x_i, false)} \qquad \text{(Eq. 12-4)}$$

This is an approximation for the probability of some specific outcome i occurring. We can convert this approximated probability into an expected frequency value $(f_{e(i)})$ via the following, where m is the number of observations in the data set:

$$f_{e(i)} = mP(x_i) \qquad \text{(Eq. 12-5)}$$

At this point, we are able to conduct our chi-square test because we have values of f_o and f_e for all possible outcomes.

Let us illustrate chi-square testing for a normal distribution via an example. Let us suppose that a company makes medication in 20mg tablets. The company claims variation on the size of the tablets, but says they have a mean mass of 20mg, with a standard deviation of 0.25mg. The company's quality control department randomly selected 361 tablets and measured their mass to the nearest 0.1mg. These possible outcomes and observed frequencies (f_o) are shown in the first two columns of Table 12-3. Given that we have f_o values, we direct our attention to finding f_e values. We start with Eq. 12-3 and 12-4 to compute first normal density values and then convert them to probabilities. These values are shown in the third and fourth columns of Table 12-3. We then convert the probabilities of the various outcomes by multiplying the probabilities by $m = 361$ total observations. This results in our expected frequencies (f_e) shown in the fifth column of Table 12-3. From here, we can calculate our χ^2 statistic, which the sixth column of Table 12-3 shows us to be 24.07. Using the "chidist" function, we learn that this test has a p-value of 0.0639. As such, for any value of α that is less than 0.0639, we can claim that the mass of the tablets are normally distributed.

Outcome	f_o	$f(x_i)$	$P(x_i)$	f_e	$(f_o-f_e)^2/f_e$
19.4	6	0.09	0.01	3.25	2.33
19.5	6	0.22	0.02	7.83	0.43
19.6	18	0.44	0.04	16.09	0.23
19.7	37	0.78	0.08	28.17	2.77
19.8	49	1.16	0.12	42.02	1.16
19.9	48	1.47	0.15	53.42	0.55
20.0	56	1.60	0.16	57.87	0.06
20.1	38	1.47	0.15	53.42	4.45
20.2	41	1.16	0.12	42.02	0.02
20.3	29	0.78	0.08	28.17	0.02
20.4	20	0.44	0.04	16.09	0.95
20.5	8	0.22	0.02	7.83	0.00
20.6	2	0.09	0.01	3.25	0.48
20.7	1	0.03	0.00	1.15	0.02
20.8	1	0.01	0.00	0.35	1.24
20.9	1	0.00	0.00	0.09	9.36
Sum	361	9.96	1		24.07

Table 12.3. Calculations for Normality Test

Figure 12-2 shows a combined histogram for Chi-Square test for normality.

Figure 12-2. Chi-Square Test for Normality

We can also test whether or not some given distribution is binomial. This is easier than testing for normality, because the binomial distribution is discrete by nature, and making an approximation from continuous to discrete is not needed here. Given a data set of observed frequencies (f_o), we can estimate the probability of success (p), and then use the binomial distribution to determine f_e values for our chi-square test.

Consider an example of a semi-retired doctor who practices medicine in a rural area. He has five appointments per day. At the end of the day, the office manager maintains a tally of patients seen on time. For example, if there is a certain day where the doctor sees two patients on time, the tally for two patients seen on time is incremented by one. Table 12.4 shows the last 100 days of on-time performance:

On-Time	0	1	2	3	4	5
Frequency (f_o)	22	26	34	11	5	2

Table 12.4. Summary of Patients Seen On-Time

We would like to know if this data follows a binomial distribution. Since we are not given the probability of success for a patient being seen on-time, we need to estimate this value. We can do this by first determining the number of patients seen on time: 0(22) + 1(26) + 2(34) + 3(11) + 4(5) + 5(2), which is

157. Since there was 500 total patients seen (5 patients/day over 100 days), the probability of a patient being seen on time is 157 / 500, which is 0.314. This value is used in the "binom.dist" function, which will provide us with probabilities associated with the number of "successes" from 0 to 5 patients being seen on time. For a reminder of the binom.dist function, please refer to distributions chapter. Using this function, along with multiplying each of these binomial probabilities by 100 days, we have the following:

Successes	0	1	2	3	4	5
f_o	22	26	34	11	5	2
Binomial Prob.	0.15	0.35	0.32	0.15	0.03	0.00
f_e	15.19	34.77	31.83	14.57	3.33	0.31
$(f_e-f_o)^2/f_e$	3.05	2.21	0.15	0.87	0.83	9.41

Table 12.5. Chi-Square Test Results for On-Time Visits

The values in the bottom row of Table 12.5 result in a χ^2 statistic of 16.53, with an associated p-value of 0.0055. At any credible value of α, we would reject H_0, and claim that the binomial distribution does not describe the given data set. Figure 12.3 shows the non-matching histograms, supporting our decision to reject H_0.

Figure 12.3. Chi-Square Test for On-Time Doctor Visits

12.3   Test for Independence

When performing goodness of fit tests, we are essentially comparing an observed set of outcomes with an expected set of outcomes. We can take this mindset further and explore whether or not multiple entities are related. What is meant by this is that we can determine whether or not multiple seemingly unrelated entities are in fact related. We can use our chi-square test approach to explore this – we call this a test for independence. In the context of H₀ and Hₐ, we state the following:

H₀: Multiple entities are independent of each other   (Eq. 12-6)
Hₐ: Multiple entities are dependent on each other

To explore what we can do for a test of independence, let us re-visit Table 4.1, where we have a breakdown of voting on a congressional bill by political party. Voting details have been omitted, and only row and column totals are shown, along with percentages

	Yes	No	Total
Republican			242 (56.94%)
Democrat			183 (43.06%)
Total	275 (64.71%)	150 (35.29%)	425

Table 12.6. House Vote Template on HR 1599

Because I know that 64.71% voted "Yes," and 56.94% are Republicans, I *expect* that (64.71%*56.94%*425) 156.59 of the 425 voters are Republicans that voted "Yes."

Formally, this expected frequency value is as follows:

$$f_{e_{(ij)}} = m\left(\frac{\sum row_i}{m}\right)\left(\frac{\sum col_j}{m}\right)$$ (Eq. 12-7)

Using Eq. 12-7, we can compute the remaining values of Table 8.6 as follows:

	Yes	No
Republican	156.59	85.41
Democrat	118.41	64.59

Table 12.7. "Expected" House Vote on HR 1599

The values in the four "filled" cells of Table 12.7 are based on expectation only – they are independent of political party and/or the actual vote – expected values. The observed values (f_o) are the original values from Table 4.1

	Yes	No
Republican	230	12
Democrat	45	138

Table 12.8. "Observed" House Vote on HR 1599

Revising our formula from Eq 12-2 to determine the test statistic for a chi-square test for independence, we have the following:

$$\chi^2 = \sum_{i=1}^{rows} \sum_{j=1}^{cols} \frac{\left(f_{o(ij)} - f_{e(ij)}\right)^2}{f_{e(ij)}}$$ (Eq. 12-8)

Using Eq. 12-8, we have the following values that need to be summed:

	Yes	No
Republican	34.42	63.10
Democrat	45.51	83.44

Table 12.9. χ^2 Calculation for House Vote on HR 1599

These values sum to 226.47. A chi-square test for independence has degrees of freedom determined as follows:

$$df = (rows - 1)(columns - 1)$$ (Eq. 12-9)

Our test, then, as (2 - 1)(2 - 1) = 1 degree of freedom. This yields a p-value < 0.0001, strongly suggesting that our two entities are not independent of each other. In other words, political party and the actual vote are related to each other, which given our political climate of strong partisanship, this should not be a surprise.

As another example, let's consider a survey completed by university students. These students were asked a question about how optimistic they are about the future. There are three possible responses: Optimistic; Indifferent; and Pessimistic. The survey respondents are also grouped according to class: freshman; sophomore; junior and senior. The observed data ($f_{o(ij)}$) are as follows:

	Fresh.	Soph.	Jr	Sr	Sum
Optimistic	7	3	2	8	20
Indifferent	6	8	9	7	30
Pessimistic	15	15	14	6	50
Sum	28	26	25	21	100

Table 12.10. Observed Frequencies for Example

The expected values are as follows:

	Fresh.	Soph.	Jr.	Sr.	Sum
Optimistic	5.60	5.20	5.00	4.20	20
Indifferent	8.40	7.80	7.50	6.30	30
Pessimistic	14.00	13.00	12.50	10.50	50
Sum	28	26	25	21	100

Table 12.11. Expected Frequencies for Example

Table 12-12 shows the components of the chi-square test statistic for independence.

	Fresh.	Soph.	Jr.	Sr
Optimistic	0.35	0.93	1.80	3.44
Indifferent	0.69	0.01	0.30	0.08
Pessimistic	0.07	0.31	0.18	1.93

Table 12.12. χ^2 Statistic Details for Example Problem

The χ^2 test statistic sums to 10.08. This test has $(3 - 1)(4 - 1) = 6$ degrees of freedom, resulting in a p-value of 0.1215. As such we fail to reject the H_0 and we claim that the entities of the student's opinion and class are independent – they are not related.

12.4   Conclusions

The chi-square test is a powerful, yet simple statistical test. Because of its simplicity, it can be used to make a variety of general determinations. The general intent of this test is to compare the observed data we are provided to the outcomes we expect. When we do this, we can address many important issues of a statistical nature.

In the next chapter, we cover simple linear regression – one of the more important concepts in statistics. With careful data preparation, we can replace regression hypothesis testing with a chi-square test. The motivation to do this is to simplify the process. This is only mentioned as an example of the value of the chi-square test. The power of the chi-square test is its simplicity.

Because of its simplicity and versatility, the chi-square test has the drawback of being somewhat unstructured. Because of this, we sometimes need to conceptualize how we will relate the observed frequencies to the expected frequencies.

12.5 Exercises

1. I flip a coin 103 times, and tails is the result 57 times. At the $\alpha = 0.05$ level, is the coin fair?
2. I roll a pair of dice 1000 times, and the following outcomes result. At the $\alpha = 0.05$ level, are the dice fair?

Outcome	2	3	4	5	6
Freq.	25	56	83	112	145

Outcome	7	8	9	10	11	12
Freq.	172	136	108	86	51	26

Use the following data for Problems 3 – 7. I flip a coin 10 times, and I tally the number times I end up with tails. I repeat this experiment 1,000 times, and end up with the following frequency for tails.

Tails	0	1	2	3	4	5
Freq.	1	5	47	115	207	248

Tails	5	6	7	8	9	10
Freq.	248	202	120	41	12	2

3. At the $\alpha = 0.05$ level, does the data reflect a binomial distribution?
4. At the $\alpha = 0.05$ level, does the data reflect a normal distribution?

5. At the α = 0.05 level, can we claim a binomial distribution with a probability of tails being 0.5?

6. At the α = 0.05 level, can we claim a normal distribution with an expected value of 5 and a standard deviation of 1.5811?

7. At the α = 0.05, is the coin fair?

8. Consider a company that manufactures lawn mowers. They make the same amount of mowers each day. At the completion of the manufacturing the mowers, the Quality Control department make a final inspection. Below is the average number of daily rejects over the past year.

Day	Mon	Tue	Wed	Thu	Fri
Rejects	21	25	19	22	31

At the α = 0.04 level, are the number of daily reject as expected?

9. Consider a large university with seven colleges. Each year, the number of cheating cases for each college are published by the university. The relevant data is as follows:

School	Cheating Cases	Enrollment
Architecture	6	1,500
Business	51	6,000
Engineering	11	6,000
Liberal Arts	6	1,500
Social Sciences	10	4,000
Sciences	15	4,000
Veterinary Medicine	1	1,000

At the α = 0.05 level, are cheating cases representative of enrollment by college?

10. People were randomly selected across the US to ask if they would like to see gun laws made more restrictive. Specifically, the question was "would you like to see gun laws in the US made more restrictive?" Both men and women were asked the question and the results are below:

	Yes	No
Men	74	51
Women	80	32

Using α = 0.03, are gender and the response to the question independent?

11. Several Americans were randomly selected and asked if they approved of the US Supreme Court's decision to permit same-sex marriage. The respondents were broken into political party affiliation. The data is shown below:

	Democrat	Unafflilated	Republican
Approve	96	31	41
Indifferent	41	42	56
Disapprove	12	38	107

Using α = 0.06, are party affiliation and the approval to same-sex marriage indepe

13.   Mathematical Programming

Up to this point, we have essentially covered data analysis. That is, we've been given data, we study the data, then we attempt to put the data in perspective – we would like to say something interesting about the data. We take a completely different tack in this, our final chapter.

Here, we are given some basic information, such as unit profit or unit cost for specific entities, a set of rules to follow, and aggregate this information such that some objective is optimized, such as maximization of profit or minimization of cost.

The process of doing this is called mathematical programming, and it requires us to build a model to optimize. This process is radically different from everything else covered to this point.

13.1   Introduction

To illustrate how mathematical programming works, we will start with a simple example. Consider a furniture company that makes two different types of chairs: Model A and Model B. Each unit of Model A results in a profit of $7/chair, while each unit of Model B results in a profit of $5/chair. When each unit of Model A is made, two assembly hours are required, and six finishing hours are required. When each unit of Model B is made, one assembly hour is required, and seven finishing hours are required. Each week, 1,600 assembly hours are available, and 8,400 finishing hours are available.

The relevant question then becomes how many units of Model A and Model B should be made such that the company's total weekly profit is maximized?

13.2   Linear Programming

The problem above has a few salient features that are noteworthy. First of all, there is a clearly-defined objective (maximize total profit). Secondly, there are entities in which the user has some control (the number of units of Models A and B to make). Finally, there are rules requiring adherence (limited assembly and finishing capacity).

These three salient features present themselves in mathematical programming problems. We must take this information and convert it into a mathematical model. This process is called **formulation**. When formulating a mathematical programming problem, we first take the entities over which we control and convert them into **decision variables**. These decision variables quantify the entities we control. For this example, we state our decision variables as follows:

x_A = the number of units of Model A to produce
x_B = the number of units of Model B to produce

Next, we consider the our objective to maximize our total profit, bearing in mind that we make $7 for each unit of Model A, and $5 for each unit of Model B. Combining the unit profits with the associated decision variables, we have the **objective function**, which in this case is to be maximized:

$$\text{Max: } 7x_A + 5x_B \qquad (13\text{-}1)$$

The last major hurdle of our effort involves converting the rules we must obey into mathematical form. For assembly, we must realize that each unit of Model A requires two hours of assembly labor, and each unit of Model B requires one hour of assembly labor, and we are limited to 1,600 total assembly hours in a one-week period. From a mathematical perspective we construct a **constraint**, and it is as follows:

$$2x_A + 1x_B \leq 1,600 \text{ (Assembly Hours)} \qquad (13\text{-}2)$$

Using similar logic for the finishing constraint, we realize that each unit of Model A requires six hours of finishing, and each unit of Model B requires seven hours of finishing, and we have 8,400 finishing hours available for our one-week period, we can construct the following finishing constraint:

$$6x_A + 7x_B \leq 8,400 \text{ (Finishing Hours)} \qquad (13\text{-}3)$$

Finally, we must state that our decision variables are not permitted to take on negative values. These non-negativity constraints are stated as follows:

$$x_A, x_B \geq 0 \text{ (Non-Negativity Constraints)} \qquad (13\text{-}4)$$

We have now formulated the problem at hand. Typically, we present the entire formulation in concise format as follows:

$$\text{Max: } 7x_A + 5x_B$$
$$\text{Subject to:}$$
$$2x_A + 1x_B \leq 1,600 \text{ (Assembly Hours)} \qquad (13\text{-}5)$$
$$6x_A + 7x_B \leq 8,400 \text{ (Finishing Hours)}$$
$$x_A, x_B \geq 0 \text{ (Non-Negativity Constraints)}$$

The words "Subject to" always imply a subsequent set of "rules" that must be followed.

The above is a formulation of a Linear Programming problem. The word "linear" is included because the objective function and all constraints are in linear form. This is not always the case, but it is the most basic and understandable form of mathematical programming.

At this point, we have formulated our problem, but we have yet to make any progress regarding our optimal, or "best" solution.

13.3 Solver

Solving mathematical programming problems is an entire field within itself, and is far beyond the scope of this book. This field is typically referred to as "Operations Research" or "Management Science," and these fields are very mathematically intense. Fortunately, Microsoft Excel can be used to solve the most basic types of problems. Specifically, there is a built-in Excel tool called "Solver" that can assist in finding the optimal solution.

Before invoking Solver, the problem must be put into Excel is spreadsheet form. There are countless ways to do this, but some sort of structured effort simplifies the process. Figure 13-1 details how our example problem was inputted into Excel.

	A	B	C	D	E	F
1		Model A	Model B		Total	
2	Quantity	0	0		$ -	
3	Unit Profit	$ 7	$ 5			
4					LHS	RHS
5	Assembly	2	1		0	1,600
6	Finishing	6	7		0	8,400
7						
8	E2: =SUMPRODUCT(B3:C3,B2:C2)					
9	E5: =SUMPRODUCT(B5:C5,B2:C2)					
10	E6: =SUMPRODUCT(B6:C6,B2:C2)					

Figure 13.1. Excel Formulation for Example Problem

The spreadsheet organizes Model A and Model B data into separate columns, while decision variable values ("Quantity"), unit profit values, assembly and finishing constraint data are detailed in rows. Coefficients are inputted in the corresponding cells. It is good practice to color-code decision variable cells and the objective function cell. For this example, decision variables are coded yellow, while the objective function value is teal. There are three cells which display calculated results: E2 for the total profit; E5 for the assembly hours consumed; and E6 for the finishing hours consumed. These formulae details are displayed above – they are the Excel version of the objective function and the left-hand side (LHS) of the two constraints. The right hand side (RHS) constraint values are shown in the appropriate cells. Such is the formulation of the problem at hand.

To actually "solve" the problem, we invoke Solver via the "Data" menu option. The Solver box displays, and we are ready to tell Solver our problem details. Figure 13.2. shows the Solver box, with all required input provided.

Figure 13.2. Solver for Example Problem

To provide Solver with the required information, we first need to tell Solver which cell contains the objective function value. In our case it is E2 (the teal cell in our example). Next we need to let Solver know which type of objective we have. In our case, we wish to maximize our objective function, so we select "Max." Next, we need to tell Solver about our decision variables. As such, when prompted with "By Changing Variable Cells," we simply select the range of cells that are decision variables (the yellow cells in our example). Next we need to add our constraints. In order to do that, we click the "Add" button in the "Subject to the Constraints" section. When we do this, we see a new box appear, similar to the one shown in Figure 13.3.

Figure 13.3. Adding a Constraint

To complete this box, we enter the left-hand-side (LHS) value in the box for "Cell Reference" and the right-hand-side (RHS) value in the box for "Constraint." The "type" of constraint must also be selected from the drop-down box – for our example, we have a "≤" type. Figure 13.3 shows details for our "Assembly Labor" constraint. When finished, we click "Add" so that we can proceed similarly for the "Finishing Labor" constraint. When finished with that, we click the OK button, which will return us to the Solver form shown in Figure 13.2.

Next, the box should be checked when asked "Make Unconstrained Variables Non-Negative." This ensures that our decision variables will not be permitted to assume negative values (non-negativity constraints). Finally, the Solving Method should be "Simplex LP." This choice uses the traditional method for solving linear programming problems.

At this point, the "Solve" button should be clicked. After receiving a message stating that Solver was successful in finding an optimal solution, the spreadsheet will display the optimal solution. Figure 13.4 shows what we have for our example problem.

	A	B	C	D	E	F
1		Model A	Model B		Total	
2	Quantity	350	900		$6,950	
3	Unit Profit	$ 7	$ 5			
4					LHS	RHS
5	Assembly	2	1		1600	1,600
6	Finishing	6	7		8400	8,400
7						
8	E2: =SUMPRODUCT(B3:C3,B2:C2)					
9	E5: =SUMPRODUCT(B5:C5,B2:C2)					
10	E6: =SUMPRODUCT(B6:C6,B2:C2)					

Figure 13.4. Optimized Solution for Example Problem

From inspection of Figure 13.4, we see that our optimal solution. We are told that 350 units of Model A and 900 units of Model B provide us our maximized total profit of $6,950. As we examine our constraints, we see that our constraints have not been violated – we have used all of our available assembly hours and finishing hours.

Solver gives us the ability to solve mathematical programming problems in Excel. Experience has suggested that converting a problem from a mathematical formulation to Excel formulation does take some practice. From this point forward, Solver will not be detailed in example problems. Instead, only mathematical formulations will be shown. Nevertheless, all mathematical programming problems covered in this chapter are available with the data sets.

13.4   Other Linear Programming Problem Types

The example problem above is probably the most basic type of linear programming problem. There are, however, many general types of linear programming problems, that run the gamut from trivial to quite complex. This section will detail a few of the most common types of linear programming problems.

13.4.1 Assignment Problem

Consider a problem where we need to assign four different factory workers to four different jobs. Each worker has some varying degree of skill at each specific job. For convenience, we will use an hourly cost to quantify a worker's skill level for a specific job – the higher the worker's skill level, the lower the hourly cost. The overall objective is to assign the four workers to the four jobs such that the total hourly cost is minimized. Consider the following cost table:

Worker\Job	Assembly	Delivery	Repair	Welding
Al	18	5	14	16
Billy	12	9	7	14
Chris	10	16	6	8
Dave	14	12	18	9

Table 13.1. Cost Table for Assignment Problem

For example, if Chris were assigned to the welding job, $8/hour would be contributed to the total cost.

The mathematical formulation for this problem is reasonably straightforward. First, the decision variables are assigned in a tabular fashion via the following:

$$x_{ij} = 1 \text{ if worker } i \text{ assigned to job } j; 0 \text{ otherwise} \qquad (13\text{-}6)$$

As this point, the binary nature of the decision variables should not be worrisome – this is addressed shortly. The objective function then multiplies the decision variables with their corresponding coefficients. Mathematically, this is as follows:

$$\text{Min: } 18x_{11} + 5x_{12} + 14x_{13} + \ldots + 9x_{44} \qquad (13\text{-}7)$$

Because each worker must be assigned to exactly one job, we have the following constraints:

$$
\begin{aligned}
&\text{Subject to:}\\
&x_{11} + x_{12} + x_{13} + x_{14} = 1 \text{ (Al)}\\
&x_{21} + x_{22} + x_{23} + x_{24} = 1 \text{ (Billy)} \qquad (13\text{-}8)\\
&x_{31} + x_{32} + x_{33} + x_{34} = 1 \text{ (Chris)}
\end{aligned}
$$

$$x_{41} + x_{42} + x_{43} + x_{44} = 1 \text{ (Dave)}$$

Likewise, each job must be assigned exactly one worker. Mathematically, we can state this as follows:

$$x_{11} + x_{21} + x_{31} + x_{41} = 1 \text{ (Assembly)}$$
$$x_{12} + x_{22} + x_{32} + x_{42} = 1 \text{ (Delivery)}$$
$$x_{13} + x_{23} + x_{33} + x_{43} = 1 \text{ (Repair)}$$
$$x_{14} + x_{24} + x_{34} + x_{44} = 1 \text{ (Welding)}$$

(13-9)

An optimal solution to this problem is to assignment Al to Delivery, Bill to Repair, Chris to Assembly, and Dave to Welding, for a total hourly cost of $5 + +$7 + $10 + $9 = $31. These costs associated with these assignments are italicized in the cost table above. We are not prepared to say that this is the optimal solution, we can only say this is an optimal solution. There could be multiple solutions resulting in a minimized cost of $31, but we are certain that $31 is in fact the minimized cost.

A comment above was made about the "binary" nature of the decision variables. The decision variables end up being binary – that is, they take on values of 0 or 1 because the constraints all sum to one, forcing a single value of "1" in each row and column. Further discussion of these specific mathematics is left for a more comprehensive course.

It should be noted that this formulation can be generalized into a more compact form, shows as follows:

$$Min: \sum_{i=1}^{n} \sum_{j=1}^{n} c_{ij} x_{ij}$$

Subject to:

$$\sum_{j=1}^{n} x_{ij} = 1, \forall i,$$

(13-10)

$$\sum_{i=1}^{n} x_{ij} = 1, \forall j$$

The c_{ij} values are simply the cost coefficients associated with assigning worker i to job j. The first set of constraints force each worker to be assigned to a single job, while the second set of constraints force each job to have one worker.

13.4.2 Transportation Problem

Another important linear programming problem is the Transportation Problem. Here, we are given some number (n) of supply sources that must ship products to some number (m) of destinations at minimal cost. The supply sources have limited capacity, and the destinations have a demand that must be met.

Table 13.2 details a Transportation Problem, with four sources and five destinations. The demand (in units) for each destination appears in the bottom row. The per-unit shipping costs are provided in the top four rows. For example, it costs $20 to ship one unit from Greensboro to Duck. Each source has a capacity of supplying 1,800 units. We wish to ship such that demand is met for all destinations without exceeding supply at a minimal cost.

Source \ Destination	Asheville	Duck	Durham	Gastonia	Raleigh
Winston-Salem	10	25	8	7	9
Charlotte	12	26	9	3	11
Greensboro	13	20	7	8	8
High Point	14	21	6	9	7
Demand	800	300	1,000	900	2,000

Table 13.2. Cost and Demand Detail for Transportation.

The formulation for this problem shares some similarities with that of the Assignment Problem. First we define our decision variables:

$$x_{ij} = \text{units shipped from source i to destination j} \qquad (13\text{-}11)$$

This provides us with the following objective function:

$$\text{Min: } 10x_{12} + 25x_{12} + \ldots + 7x_{45} \qquad (13\text{-}12)$$

In order for the supply not be exceeded for each source, we must provide the following constraints:

Subject to:

$$x_{11} + x_{12} + x_{13} + x_{14} + x_{15} \leq 1{,}800 \text{ (Winston-Salem)}$$
$$x_{21} + x_{22} + x_{23} + x_{24} + x_{25} \leq 1{,}800 \text{ (Charlotte)} \qquad (13\text{-}13)$$
$$x_{31} + x_{32} + x_{33} + x_{34} + x_{35} \leq 1{,}800 \text{ (Greensboro)}$$

$$x_{41} + x_{42} + x_{43} + x_{44} + x_{45} \leq 1{,}800 \text{ (High Point)}$$

The demand constraints are as follows:

$$x_{11} + x_{21} + x_{31} + x_{41} = 800 \text{ (Asheville)}$$
$$x_{12} + x_{22} + x_{32} + x_{42} = 300 \text{ (Duck)}$$
$$x_{13} + x_{23} + x_{33} + x_{43} = 1{,}000 \text{ (Durham)} \qquad (13\text{-}14)$$
$$x_{14} + x_{24} + x_{34} + x_{44} = 900 \text{ (Gastonia)}$$
$$x_{15} + x_{25} + x_{35} + x_{45} = 2{,}000 \text{ (Raleigh)}$$

Table 13.3 shows the optimal distribution from the sources to the destinations. The minimized cost is $37,900

Source \ Destination	Asheville	Duck	Durham	Gastonia	Raleigh
Winston-Salem	800	0	0	0	0
Charlotte	0	0	0	900	0
Greensboro	0	300	0	0	1,200
High Point	0	0	1,000	0	800

Table 13.3. Optimal Distribution for Transportation Problem

As is the case with the Assignment Problem, the Transportation Problem can also be generalized into the following form:

$$Min: \sum_{i=1}^{n}\sum_{j=1}^{m} c_{ij}x_{ij}$$

Subject to:

$$\sum_{j=1}^{m} x_{ij} \leq Supply_i, \forall i, \qquad (13\text{-}15)$$

$$\sum_{i=1}^{n} x_{ij} = Demand_j, \forall j$$

13.4.3 Blending Problem

The last type of linear programming problem discussed is the blending problem. The blending problem is where there is a need to combine ingredients into some finished product in a minimal cost or maximal profit fashion. These problems are typically more challenging to formulate than the ones previously discussed.

As an example, consider a company that combines two different components into three different animal feeds. The first component is a protein source, while the second is a carbohydrate source. Feed 1 must be at least 25% protein, and sells for $1.45/pound. Feed 2 must be at least 40% protein, and sells for $1.52/pound. Feed 3 must be at least 55% protein and sells for $1.60/pound. Component 1 costs $1.05/pound and the weekly supply is limited to 5,000 pounds. Component 2 costs $0.25/pound and the weekly supply is limited to 6,500 pounds. Demand for each of the three feeds is assumed to be unlimited. Our job is to mix the component for each of the three feeds such that the company's total profit is maximized.

This problem is more difficult to formulate as compared to the others covered. There are several ways to proceed, but the approach chosen here is believed to be the least complex. Let us first realize that there are two inputs (Protein and Carbohydrate sources) and three outputs (Feeds A, B and C). A decision variable will be defined for each input/output combination. As such, our decision variables are defined as follows:

$$x_{ij} = \text{pounds of component i used for feed j} \qquad (13\text{-}16)$$

Specific decision variable names and other relevant problem data are organized in Table 13.4.

	Feed A	Feed B	Feed C	Supply	Unit Cost
Comp. 1 (Protein)	x_{1A}	x_{1B}	x_{1C}	5,000	$1.05
Comp. 2 (Carb.)	x_{2A}	x_{2B}	x_{2C}	6,500	$0.25
Protein Minimum	25%	40%	55%		
Unit Profit	$1.45	$1.52	$1.60		

Table 13.4. Data for Blending Problem

To formulate the objective function, it must be realized that in order to maximize profit, we must maximize the difference between revenue and cost. In the context of this problem, the objective function is as follows:

$$\text{Max: } [1.45(x_{1A} + x_{2A}) + 1.52(x_{1B} + x_{2B}) + 1.60(x_{1C} + x_{2C})] \qquad (13\text{-}17)$$
$$- [1.05(x_{1A} + x_{1B} + x_{1C}) + 0.25(x_{2A} + x_{2B} + x_{2C})]$$

The first part of the objective function is revenue, while the second part is cost. The supply constraints are more straightforward:

Subject to:

$$x_{1A} + x_{1B} + x_{1C} \leq 5{,}000 \text{ (Protein Component)} \qquad (13\text{-}18)$$
$$x_{2A} + x_{2B} + x_{2C} \leq 6{,}500 \text{ (Carb. Component)}$$

The protein constraints can be constructed by relating the actual ratio of protein weight to total weight for each feed. This is done as follows:

$$x_{1A}/(x_{1A} + x_{2A}) \geq 0.25$$
$$x_{1B}/(x_{1B} + x_{2B}) \geq 0.40 \qquad (13\text{-}19)$$
$$x_{1C}/(x_{1C} + x_{2C}) \geq 0.55$$

There is, however, a problem with these three constraints. They are nonlinear – there are decision variables in the numerator, which complicates the solution process. With some algebraic manipulation, however, they can be restored to linear form. When both sides of the constraints are multiplied by the denominator on the left-hand side, linear form is restored:

$$x_{1A} \geq 0.25(x_{1A} + x_{2A})$$
$$x_{1B} \geq 0.40(x_{1B} + x_{2B}) \qquad (13\text{-}20)$$
$$x_{1C} \geq 0.55(x_{1C} + x_{2C})$$

The problem is now formulated, and Solver provides the following result with a maximized profit of $10,862.50.

	Feed A	Feed B	Feed C
Comp. 1 (Protein)	1104.17	0	3895.83
Comp. 2 (Carb.)	3312.50	0	3187.50

Table 13.5. Optimal Solution to the Blending Problem

Solver determined that Feed B should not be made.

13.5   Integer Programming

When solving mathematical programming problems, there are times when it is necessary to guarantee our decision variables take on integer values. The example above shows a solution with non-integer decision variable values. Perhaps it is only possible to buy in one-pound units. As such, we would need to ensure our decision variables take on integer values.

Another relevant scenario is when we would like our optimal solution to decide whether or not a certain condition applies in our optimal solution. In other words, we would like to have the ability to impose certain logical scenarios in our effort to find an optimal solution.

Both of these scenarios can be addressed by a mathematical programming concept referred to as integer programming. The first type of integer programming is where we mandate certain decision variables to take on integer values, such as 0, 1, 2, ..., whereas the second scenario mandates that certain decision variables take on binary values – that is, values that are either 0 or 1. This second scenario might sound trivial on the surface, but binary variable add great power and flexibility to mathematical programming models.

13.5.1 Integer Decision Variables

As can be seen in Table 13.5, our optimal solution for the blending problem yields a non-integer solution. If it is not possible to purchase the components in partial pounds, it would be in our best interest to optimize when our decision variables are restricted to integer values. In Excel/Solver, this is straightforward to do. We need to add a constraint to classify all decision variables to take on integer values. This is illustrated in Figure 13.5.

Figure 13.5. Stating Integer Variables for Blending Problem

In the Constraints section, we click "Add." We then select the decision variables we wish to restrict as integer, and then select "int" in the drop-down box. We then click "OK" and then choose "Solve." Our new optimal solution is shown in Table 13.6.

	Feed A	Feed B	Feed C
Comp. 1 (Protein)	1104	2	3894
Comp. 2 (Carb.)	3311	3	3186

Table 13.6. Optimal Solution to the Blending Problem

One should note that enforcing decision variables to take on integer values is not necessarily a matter of "rounding" variables accordingly. Decision variables can change to some significant degree. It is also worth noting that our maximized profit is now $10,862.35 – a small decrease from the earlier solution. Given that constraints have been added to this problem, we can only expect the optimized objective function value to worsen.

13.5.2 Binary Variables

The other salient feature in using integer variables is when we restrict decision variables to take on one of two possible values: zero or one. Such variables are called "binary" variables.[10] The use of binary variables enables us to induce logical conditions in our model building.

As a simple example of binary variables, consider the following scenario: A large construction is budgeting resources for their next fiscal year, and they are considering ten potential projects. Each project has an expected return, an expected investment, and an expected labor requirement. The investment budget is limited to $12M, and the available labor is 100K hours. Details are as follows:

Potential Project	Expected Return ($M)	Expected Inv. ($M)	Expected Labor (K hours)
1	10	2.5	18
2	8	2	13
3	12	2.8	20
4	6	1.2	5
5	4	1	4
6	15	5	22
7	12	3	16
8	9	2	6

[10] In Computer Science, these variables are referred to as "Boolean Variables."

Table 13.7. Potential Projects

Additionally, no more than 5 projects are to be pursued, so as to make the high-level project management details as reasonable as possible.

It is desired, of course, that expected revenue be maximized, while simultaneously adhering to the budgets for investment expenditure and labor availability, along with the limit of five projects pursued.

In order to formulate this problem, we define a type of decision variable called "y_i," which takes on a value of either zero or one. Mathematically, we state the following:

$$y_i = 1 \text{ if project i is pursued; 0 otherwise} \qquad (13\text{-}21)$$

This means that if a project is not pursued, the binary variable takes on a value of zero, and from a mathematical standpoint, "disappears." Otherwise, if a project is pursued, and it's revenue, expense, labor and pursuance are added accordingly. This results in the following objective function:

$$\text{Max: } 10y_1 + 8y_2 + 12y_3 + 6y_4 + 4y_5 + 15y_6 + 12y_7 + 9y_8 \qquad (13\text{-}22)$$

Subject to the following constraints:

$$2.5y_1 + 2y_2 + 2.8y_3 + 1.2y_4 + 1y_5 + 5y_6 + 3y_7 + 2y_8 \le 12 \qquad (13\text{-}23)$$
$$\text{(Budget Limit)}$$

$$18y_1 + 13y_2 + 20y_3 + 5y_4 + 4y_5 + 22y_6 + 16y_7 + 6y_8 \le 100 \qquad (13\text{-}24)$$
$$\text{(Labor Limit)}$$

$$y_1 + y_2 + y_3 + y_4 + y_5 + y_6 + y_7 + y_8 \le 5 \text{ (Project Limit)} \qquad (13\text{-}25)$$

This model can easily be incorporated into Excel. The only nuance here is that the binary decision variables ($y_1 - y_8$) be characterized as binary variables. This is shown in Figure 13.6.

From Figure 13.6, we learn that Projects 1, 3, 4, 7 and 8 should be selected, and will provide an expected revenue of $49M. $11.5M will have been expended, 65K labor hours will have been used, and 5 projects will have been pursued – all of these values have complied with the constraints.

Figure 13.6. Project Planning Problem

In the above example, we essentially gave ourselves to the ability to use an on/off switch for our decision variables – projects specifically. We can also exploit binary variables to do the same to constraints. If we revisit our transportation problem from Section 13.4.2, we see that we transport from four sources to five destinations. Or more generally, we ship from n possible sources to m possible destinations. With binary variables, we have the ability to use a subset of n if we desire.

We will re-visit the transportation problem example above, and now mandate that at-most, three sources can be used. This type of problem is referred to as a "Fixed-Charge Problem." To solve, we keep all of the decision variables that we previously defined. In addition, we now define a new set of binary variables, that is follows:

$$y_i = 1 \text{ if source is used; 0 otherwise} \tag{13-26}$$

The supply constraints are now as follows:

$$x_{11} + x_{12} + x_{13} + x_{14} + x_{15} \leq 1{,}800y_1 \text{ (Winston-Salem)} \qquad (13\text{-}27)$$
$$x_{21} + x_{22} + x_{23} + x_{24} + x_{25} \leq 1{,}800y_2 \text{ (Charlotte)}$$
$$x_{31} + x_{32} + x_{33} + x_{34} + x_{35} \leq 1{,}800y_3 \text{ (Greensboro)}$$
$$x_{41} + x_{42} + x_{43} + x_{44} + x_{45} \leq 1{,}800y_4 \text{ (High Point)}$$

In the event that the binary variable is one, the constraint behaves as it normally would. When the binary variable is zero, the constraint's right-hand side is forced to zero, which forces all associated decision variables on the left-hand side to equal zero. Hence, the constraint would essentially "disappear."

The demand constrains do not change in this type of formulation. One last constraint is needed to complete the formulation, which limits the transportation sources to three. This is as follows:

$$y_1 + y_2 + y_3 + y_4 \leq 3 \text{ (three source limit)} \qquad (13\text{-}28)$$

This problem is solved in Excel, and the optimal distribution is as follows:

Source \ Destination	Asheville	Duck	Durham	Gastonia	Raleigh
Winston-Salem	0	0	0	0	0
Charlotte	800	0	0	900	0
Greensboro	0	300	1,000	0	200
High Point	0	0	0	0	1,800

Table 13.8. Optimal Distribution for Fixed-Charge Problem

The minimized cost is $39,500. It should be noted that Winston-Salem is not a distribution source. There are only three distribution sources, which adheres to the new constraint. It should also be noted that the minimized cost here is inferior to the minimized cost of the earlier transportation problem ($37,900). This should not be surprising – a constraint has been added, subsequently reducing our ability to find the "best" solution.

13.6   Conclusions

Linear programming is a powerful tool in the world of Quantitative Analysis. We build models to assist us in making optimal decisions. This enhances the competitive position of the organization. Optimization models are prevalent in today's world. UPS, FedEx, the US Postal Service, airlines, and railway systems, public utilities are always trying to make optimal decisions regarding the large-scale and complex variety of services they provide.

Linear Programming is the introductory building block to the larger field of "Operations Research," which came into existence during the Industrial Revolution of the early Twentieth Century. At this point in time, economies of scale increased to the point where it was deemed important to pursue all possible gains in efficiency.

Unlike statistics, where a data set is analyzed, Linear Programming essentially starts with a "blank piece of paper" and are asked to build a model to optimize something – this is both intimidating and complicated. It only gets easier with experience.

As stated, Linear Programming is the first step into Operations Research. Subsequent important topics include nonlinear optimization, network optimization and optimal decision-making in the presence of uncertainly.

13.7 Problems

1. The owner of a ranch is trying to determine how to blend two types of animal feed. For the purposes of this exercise, we will call these Feed A and Feed B. Feed A costs $0.50/pound, while Feed B costs $0.75/pound. These two animal feeds contain five essential ingredients which need to be present to some degree in the feed mixture. Details of these five essential ingredients, along with their minimum daily requirements are shown below:

Ingredient	Feed A	Feed B	Min Daily Req. (Pounds)
1	20%	25%	30
2	30%	10%	50
3	0%	30%	20
4	24%	15%	60
5	10%	20%	40

For example, one pound of Feed A contains 0.24 pounds of Ingredient 4, while one pound of Feed B contains 0.15 pounds of Ingredient 4, and the feed mixture must yield at least 60 pounds of Ingredient 4 each day. How should Feed A and Feed B should be mixed such that the total daily cost is minimized subject to the minimum ingredient rules stated above? Formulate and solve as a mathematical programming problem.

2. MetalCo desires to blend a new alloy of 40% tin, 35% zinc, and 25% lead from five available ores having the following properties and costs:

Property	Ore 1	Ore 2	Ore 3	Ore 4	Ore 5
Tin %	60%	25%	45%	20%	50%
Zinc %	10%	15%	45%	50%	40%
Lead %	30%	60%	10%	30%	10%
Cost ($/#)	22	20	25	24	27

For example, one pound of Ore 4 yields 20% tin, 50% zinc, and 30% lead, and costs $24/pound. Your job is to find the minimum cost formulation of these five ores such that the alloy requirement is met. At least 50 pounds of each ore must be used. Formulate and solve as a mathematical programming problem.

3. I have promised a friend that I would copy the Psychedelic Furs' "Forever Now" album for them. Unfortunately, my friend does not have a CD player in their car – just a cassette tape player. Because of this, I need to put music on Side 1 of the tape, and music on Side 2 of the tape. My friend has asked that the total length of the songs be "balanced" as much as possible. By "balanced," my friend means that the total song duration on Side 1 be as close as possible to the total song duration on Side 2. The ten songs, (and their associated durations) that comprise the album are as follows:

Track #	Song	Min	Sec
1	Forever Now	5	37
2	Love My Way	3	35
3	Goodbye	3	56
4	Only You and I	4	26
5	Sleep Comes Down	3	52
6	President Gas	5	21
7	Run and Run	3	49
8	Danger	2	39
9	No Easy Street	4	9
10	Yes I Do	3	54

For example, if Songs 1 – 5 are on Side 1, the music duration will be 1286 sec, while Songs 6 – 10 will then be on Side 2, for a duration of 1192 sec, resulting in a time difference of 94 sec between the two sides. We wish to minimize this time difference. Formulate and solve as a linear programming problem.

4. Ray Bob's Oil Company (RayBobOCo) blends two types of fuel: regular and premium. These fuels are made by blending gasoline and alcohol. RayBobOCo can buy up to 100,000 barrels of gasoline/week at a cost of $80/barrel, and up to 12,000 barrels of alcohol at $94/barrel. Each barrel is equivalent to 55 gallons. Regular is made by blending nine parts of gasoline to one part alcohol. Premium is a blend of 87% gasoline and 13% alcohol. One gallon of regular sells for $2.65, while each gallon of premium sells for $2.83. The market demands at least 600,000 gallons of premium per week, and at least 1 million gallons of regular/week. Additionally, there must be at least twice as much regular produced as compared to premium. Assume that everything produced will be immediately sold. How should RayBobOCo proceed such that their profits are maximized? Formulate as a mathematical programming problem and solve.

5. A company processes coal in northeast Ohio. They grade coal into three groups: Grades A, B and C. They net a profit of $10 for each ton of Grade A, $7.5 for each ton of Grade B, $4 for each ton of Grade C. Each ton of Grade A coal requires 5 hours of processing labor and 1 hour of packaging labor. Each ton of Grade B coal requires 4 hours of processing labor and 0.75 hours of packaging labor. Each ton of Grade C coal requires 3 hours of processing labor and 0.2 hours of packaging labor. There are 100 hours of processing labor available for the next planning period, and there are 200 hours of packaging labor available for the next planning period. Grade A coal can be no more than 50% of the product mix, and Grade C must be at least 20% of the product mix. Processing fractional tons of coal is permitted. How should to the company proceed, in terms of how much of each type of coal to process, such that their profits are maximized? Formulate and solve as a mathematical programming model.

6. Billy's Trucking company specializes in shipping hazardous waste products from four sources (Bangor [Maine], Detroit, El Paso and

Oakland) to four different disposal locations (Berkeley, Boulder, Eugene, Madison). Each of these three sources has generated a quantity of waste requiring disposal (in tons). Each of the four disposal locations has a limited capacity (in tons). Each source / disposal location has a per-unit shipping cost in $/ton. Below is the pricing schedule for each source / destination combination:

	Berkeley	Boulder	Eugene	Madison	Req.
Bangor	75	55	80	40	175
Detroit	65	45	70	12	500
El Paso	50	40	60	42	125
Oakland	6	30	25	45	200
Cap.	800	1100	1200	900	

How should the hazardous waste be transported in a minimum-cost fashion? Formulate and solve as a mathematical programming problem.

7. Re-formulate Problem 6 so that only three disposal sites are permitted.

8. Re-formulated Problem 6 so that only two disposal sites are permitted.

9. Re-formulate Problem 6 so that only one disposal site is permitted.

10. Al, Billy, Cal, Dina, and Eddy are super-salespersons – they can sell anything. Although they have different personalities, they all share the characteristic of being able to sell their company's products. These five sales-persons need to be assigned to different territories. Given their personalities and cultural differences, the matrix below show the estimated sales revenues for each possible territorial assignment. These assignment revenues are as follows:

	East	Northeast	Plains	Southeast	West
Al	100	95	83	85	95
Billy	125	115	110	150	120
Cal	100	105	120	110	115
Dina	105	125	120	95	110
Eddy	110	110	115	85	115

Assign each of these super-salespersons into a territory such that total expected revenue is maximized.

11. A candidate running for the US Senate needs to visit five cities in North Carolina before the election. These five cities are: Asheville,

Charlotte, Greensboro, Raleigh and Wilmington. The candidate needs to return to the same city from which they departed, and must do so in a minimum distance fashion. Using the distance table below (in miles), formulate and solve as a mathematical programming problem.

	Ashe.	Char.	Greens.	Ral.	Wilm.
Asheville	x	131	172	247	332
Charlotte	131	x	92	166	198
Greensboro	172	92	x	76	208
Raleigh	247	166	76	x	130
Wilmington	332	198	208	130	x

12. The Sikafoos Brothers own a construction company, and are planning ahead for the next fiscal year. At present, they are considering ten potential projects. Each potential project has an expected revenue and expected cost. These potential projects are below:

Project	Expected Revenue	Expected Cost
1	$2.2M	$0.6M
2	$1.5M	$0.5M
3	$3M	$1.1M
4	$2.5M	$0.75M
5	$4M	$1M
6	$1.5M	$0.8M
7	$2.3M	$0.7M
8	$5M	$2.75M
9	$1M	$0.3M
10	$2.2M	$1M

The Sikafoos Brothers have a project budget of $5.5M for the next fiscal year. In addition to the limited budget, there are a few other rules that must be followed: Either Project 7 or Project 8 must be chosen, but not both. If Project 3 is chosen, Project 4 must also be chosen. Project 1 and Project 9 must share the same fate – either they will both be chosen, nor neither will be chosen. Your job is to formulated and solve such that total expected revenue is maximized.

13. The Barletto Brothers run a small steel furnace operation. They convert iron ore, scrap metal and refined iron into ingots. They produce two types of ingots: standard and premium. The standard

ingots sell for $1,000/ton, while the premium ingots sell for $1,200/ton. They purchase the raw materials with the following prices: iron ore is purchased for $150/ton, scrap metal is purchased for $250/ton, while refined iron is purchased for $600 per ton. For the next planning period, there is an availability of 30 tons of iron ore, 25 tons of scrap metal and 30 tons of refined iron. The standard steel is limited to 25% iron ore, limited to 55% scrap metal, and must be at least 40% refined iron. The premium steel is limited to 18% iron ore, limited to 50% scrap metal and must be at least 45% refined iron. Due to customer contracts, the Standard Steel must be at least 30% of the product-mix. Assume demand for both standard and premium steel to be unlimited. Formulate and solve a mathematical programming model such that net profit is maximized.

14. Decision Tree Analysis

Life is filled with decision-making. Some decisions are easy, some are difficult. In this chapter, we deal with the difficult decisions – at least from a quantitative standpoint. An example of an easy decision is one where we are offered two jobs – we will call them A and B. If jobs A and B are identical in every aspect, with the exception of compensation, we take the job offering the highest compensation. This decision is trivial.

Let's take this example one step further. Job A offers more compensation than does Job B, but Job B looks more promising in terms of professional growth. What is the likelihood for growth regarding Job B? How much growth is associated with Job B? All of a sudden this decision becomes less trivial because of the uncertainty associated with future professional growth opportunities. In short, we are confronted with a difficult decision.

In this chapter, we explore the tools used to analyze decisions that involved uncertainty.

14.1 Decision Trees

To address these decisions involving uncertainty, we first itemize the list of options and call them **alternatives**. We will assume there are n unique alternatives, and refer to alternative i as a_i. Each alternative has an uncertain **outcome** that does not present itself until after the decision is made. We will assume that there are m possible outcomes for each alternative. Each outcome has a certain probability of occurring. We will refer to the probability of outcome j occurring as p_j. Each outcome has an associated **payoff**. We will refer to the payoff associated with alternative i and outcome j as P_{ij}.

We combine all of this information via a decision tree – a graphical representation of all alternatives and associated outcomes and payoffs. A rectangular node represents where a decision needs to be made. A round node represents an outcome of which we are uncertain. Each outcome has some probability of occurring. After the uncertainty is represented, we are shown the payoff in monetary or similar units.

As an example, consider the decision of whether or not to bring an umbrella to work in the morning. There are two alternatives: bring an umbrella or do not bring an umbrella. For each alternative, there is uncertainty: rain or no rain. Our decision is influenced by the possible outcomes. This problem is represented by the decision tree shown in Figure 14.1

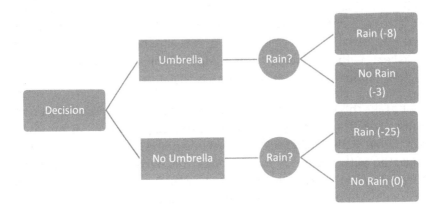

Figure 14.1. Decision Tree for Umbrella Problem

There are four outcomes for this problem: (1) we bring an umbrella and it rains; (2) we bring an umbrella and it does not rain; (3) we do not bring an umbrella and it rains; and (4) we do not bring an umbrella and it rains. The payoffs associated with these outcomes are: -8, -3 -25 and 0. These payoffs are in units of **utility** – a non-monetary unit associated with success. "Utility" is often used economics.

14.2   Decision Strategies

We are not unable to make a decision (choose an alternative) until we know what it is we wish to accomplish. As such, prior to making a decision, we need to pursue a particular strategy. In decision analysis, there are several strategies, but we will cover the three most basic here.

14.2.1 Optimistic Strategy ("Maximax")

If we are optimistic, we assume the best will happen. In this case, we choose our alternative assuming the best possible outcome will occur. This means that for each alternative, we select the most favorable outcome and then select the alternative with the best overall outcome. For our umbrella problem, then, we choose accordingly:

$$\text{Max}[\max(-8, -3), \max(-25, 0)] \qquad \text{(Eq. 14-1)}$$

This simplifies to the following:

$$\text{Max}[-3, 0] = 0 \qquad \text{(Eq. 14-2)}$$

This **"maximax"** value of 0 is the payoff associated with not bringing an umbrella, because we assume there will be no rain. The upshot of this is that under the optimistic strategy, we choose not to bring an umbrella because we don't think it is going to rain.

14.2.2 Pessimistic Strategy ("Maximin")

If we are pessimistic, we assume the worst will happen, and the make the best decision accordingly. This means that for each alternative, we assume the worst will happen, and then choose the alternative that provides us with the best result. For our umbrella problem, we proceed as follows:

$$\text{Max}[\min(-8, -3), \min(-25, 0)] \qquad \text{(Eq. 14-3)}$$

This simplifies to the following:

$$\text{Max}[-8, -25] = -8 \qquad \text{(Eq. 14-4)}$$

The **"maximin"** value here is -8, the payoff associated with bringing an umbrella when it rains. This means that the best pessimistic decision is to bring an umbrella because we think it will rain.

14.2.3 Expected Value Strategy

The first two strategies covered are important strategies, but for this example, the results are self-obviating – the optimist will not bring an umbrella because they do not think it will rain, while the pessimist will bring an umbrella because they think it will rain.

We will now examine another strategy that is more rooted in mathematics and specifically probability. We will explore the expected value strategy, which is based on what we expect each alternative's value to be. The expected value for alternative a_i is represented as $E(a_i)$ and is determined as follows:

$$E(a_i) = \sum_{j=1}^{m} p_j P_{ij} \qquad \text{(Eq. 14-5)}$$

For our umbrella problem, we will assume a probability of rain to be 0.25, which implies a probability of no rain as 0.75.

For the umbrella alternative, our expected value is:

$$(.25)(-8) + (.75)(-3) = -4.25 \qquad \text{(Eq. 14-6)}$$

For the no umbrella alternative, our expected value is:

$$(.25)(-25) + (.75)(0) = -6.25 \qquad \text{(Eq. 14-7)}$$

Comparing the expected values of the two alternatives, we wish to maximize:

$$\text{Max}[-4.25, -6.25] = -4.25 \qquad \text{(Eq. 14-8)}$$

Our best alternative has an expected value of -4.25, and is associated with the "bring umbrella alternative." As such, using expected value, we should not bring the umbrella. We will call this value of -4.25 as the **expected value**.

14.3 Expected Value of Perfect Information

We can take our discussion of expected value one step further. When we calculated our expected value (EV) above, we essentially calculated the **expected value under uncertainty** because we were not certain what would happen in the future. Let's assume for a moment that we have the ability to make our decision with advanced knowledge of what will happen. For example, if we knew in advance it was going to rain, we would bring our umbrella, and if we knew in advance it was not going to rain, we would not bring our umbrella. In terms of the mathematical approach to this problem, the **expected value under certainty** would be as follows:

$$EVUC = \sum_{j=1}^{m} p_j \cdot \max_i(P_{ij}) \qquad \text{(Eq. 14-9)}$$

For our umbrella problem, assume we have advance knowledge that it will rain. With that knowledge, we select an umbrella as that payoff is better than the payoff associated with not bringing un umbrella when it rains (max[-8, -

25] = -8). With advance knowledge that it will not rain, we would choose not to bring an umbrella because of the higher payoff (max[-3, 0] = 0). Because our advance knowledge of rain will occur 25% of the time, and advance knowledge of no rain will occur 75% of the time, our expected value under certainty value is as follows:

$$EVUC = (-8)(.25) + (0)(.75) = -2 \qquad \text{(Eq. 14-10)}$$

In other words, under certainty – with advance knowledge of what will happen, we expect a payoff of -2.

To summarize, under uncertainty, we have an expected value of -4.25. We refer to this value as the expected value, or the **expected value under uncertainty** (EVUU). Under certainty, we have an expected value of -2. We call this the expected value under certainty (EVUC). The difference between these two values is referred to as the expected value with perfect information (EVPI). Mathematically, this value is as follows:

$$EVPI = EVUC - EVUU \qquad \text{(Eq. 14-11)}$$

For our example, the EVPI is -2 - (-4.25) = 2.25. This value is always positive, and numerically represents the difference between being certain and being uncertain. Another way to interpret this is maximum amount you should "pay" to eliminate uncertainty.

14.4   An Example

Let is consider a monetary example with three investment alternatives: Bonds, Stocks and CDs. Each alternative has three possible outcomes: growth, stagnation and inflation. We assume that the probability of growth is 50%, the probability of stagnation is 30%, and the probability of inflation is 20%. Figure 14.2 shows the details of this problem, including payoffs in decision tree format.

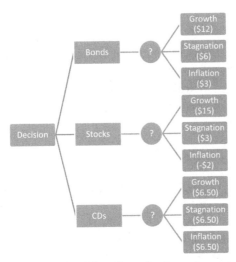

Figure 14.2. Decision Tree for Investment Problem

Table 14.1 displays this data in table format for easy calculations.

Alternative	Outcomes			Results		
	Growth (p = 0.5)	Stag. (p = 0.3)	Inflation (p = 0.2)	Max	Min	EVUU
Bonds	$12	$6	$3	$12	$3	$8.4
Stocks	$15	$3	-$2	$15	-$2	$8
CDs	$6.5	$6.5	$6.5	$6.5	$6.5	$6.5
Max Val.	$15	$6.5	$6.5	$15	$6.5	$8.4
Decision	N/A			Stocks	CDs	Bonds

Table 14.1. Details of Monetary Example Decision Tree Problem

For each alternative, the maximum, minimum and expected value payoffs have been determined. The optimist would choose Stocks because $15, the best possible outcome would occur via the Stocks decision. The pessimist would choose CDs, because $6.5 is the best outcome assuming the worst will happen. When pursuing expected value, Bonds is the best decision, because they provide the highest expected value ($8.4).

The expected value under certainty is as follows:

$$EVUC = 15(0.5) + 6.5(0.3) + 6.5(0.3) = 10.75 \qquad \text{(Eq. 14-12)}$$

Now that we understand the expected value under uncertainty is $8.4 and the expected value under certainty is $10.75, we can calculate the expected value of perfect information as ($10.75 − $8.4 = $2.35). To put this result into a monetary context, we can say that the value of eliminating uncertainty is $2.35 − if we hired someone with the ability to somehow remove uncertainty from our problem, we should pay them no more than $2.35 for their services.

14.5   Conclusions

Decision analysis is an important topic in that it bridges the theoretical and applied worlds. I have personally never constructed a decision tree for a decision that I have needed to make. Nevertheless, a decision tree does structure a decision in terms of options, associated uncertainties and their interrelationships, which is important.

Another thing worth considering is that our payoffs are subjected to interpretation. In our umbrella example, we talk about how being in the rain without an umbrella is somehow a "bad" thing. That is basically stated from the perspective of someone traveling to work or classes at the university. Imagine, however, a nervous farmer in South Dakota worried about a dried-out corn crop in August. If that farmer is caught in a downpour without an umbrella will they be upset? Of course not − they will be relieved and happy. This point needs to be made because payoffs need to be valued from the proper perspective.

Another issue to consider is the concept of outcomes. In our example problems, our outcomes are "discrete" − either a specific outcome occurs or does not occur. In reality that is not the case. For our example problem, we have outcomes that state it is either raining or it is not raining. Unfortunately, there are times, especially in places like Seattle, San Francisco or London where we are in a fog, and we're not sure if it is raining or not − such situations are not discrete. The thinking behind quantification of payoffs and outcomes is part of a larger social science known as decision/utility theory.

Finally, it is worth mentioning the concept of expected value with perfect information. As we define this concept, we describe it as the value of eliminating uncertainty. In reality, of course, we cannot eliminate uncertainty. If we had that ability, there is essentially no reason in having this book.

Nevertheless, we do perform better as organizations and individuals if we can minimize uncertainty. Consider financial service companies like ETrade and TDAmeritrade. These corporations, along with others, boast of research they provide which "reduces" uncertainty, and subsequently improving portfolio performance. They are essentially claiming that they have the ability to reduce uncertainty. Regardless of whether or not these vague claims are true, they do entice the investor to consider the value of the advertised research – the claim of reduced uncertainty, which lies at the heart of decision analysis.

14.6   Exercises

For these questions, address the following: state what the optimist would do; state what the pessimist would do; state what one would do using expected value as a strategy; and state the expected value of perfect information.

1. I have some money to invest, and I have three investment options: ChemicalBrothers, MötleyCrüe, and ConcreteBlonde. ChemicalBrothers has a payoff of $10 when a good market occurs, and a loss of $5 when a bad market occurs. MötleyCrüe has a payoff of $7 when a good market occurs, and a loss of $4 when a bad market occurs. ConcreteBlonde has a payoff of $5 when a good market occurs, and a loss of $2 when a bad market occurs. A good market has a 40% chance of occurring.

2. You have been given some money to invest, and you are considering three different options for your investment choice: AlphaStuds, BetaStuds and GammaStuds. Under a favorable market, AlphaStuds will return $100, but lose $30 under an unfavorable market. Under a favorable market, BetaStuds will return $75, but lose $25 under an unfavorable market. GammaStuds will return $60 under a favorable market, but lose $15 under an unfavorable market. A favorable market has a 60% of occurring, while an unfavorable market has a 40% chance of occurring. All money must be invested in one of the three options – distributing the investment among multiple investments is not permitted.

3. I have some money to invest. I will invest all of it in either RustStuds or JetElectro. RustStuds will return a gain of $10 in a favorable market and a loss of $3 in an unfavorable market. JetElectro will return a gain $14 in a favorable market, and a loss of $5 in an unfavorable market. The probability of the market being favorable is 60%, while there is a 40% probability of an unfavorable market.

4. I have some money to invest, and I'm considering three possible investments: AcmeCorp, BestCorp, and CoolioCorp. When the return is favorable, I can expect a $1,000 payoff from AcmeCorp, a $500 return from BestCorp, and a $400 return from CoolioCorp. When the return is unfavorable, I can expect a loss of $300 from AcmeCorp, a loss of $200 from BestCorp, and a loss of $100 from CoolioCorp. There is a 55% probability of a favorable return and a 45% probability of an unfavorable return.

5. I have $1M to invest. I have narrowed my investment choices down to two possible alternatives: AlphaTron and OmegaTron. I must invest all of the $1M in one of the securities – mixing the investment between the two securities is not permitted. Under good market conditions, AlphaTron will provide a return of $100K, while OmegaTron will provide a return of $60K. Under average market conditions, AlphaTron will provide a return of $20K, while OmegaTron will provide a return of $10K. Under bad market conditions, AlphaTron will lose $60K, while OmegaTron will lose $30K. Good market conditions are estimated to occur with a 40% probability, average and bad market conditions are each estimated to occur with a 30% probability.

Appendix. Data Repair

From a reality perspective, it is unfortunate the data sets provided with this book are "tidy." This means that there are no missing observations, and all observations have been properly measured and accounted for. In practice, this is rarely the case. Data collection is messy work, and highly prone to error and/or incompleteness. This is particularly the case when the internet is used to collect entire data sets – the data may not be fully compatible with the web-browsing software, resulting in "messy" data. Messy data is quite common with large data sets, which is nowadays often referred to as "big data."

Figure A1. Missing Data

If only a small portion of data is missing in a large data set, it is likely that removal of the data records[11] with missing data is not problematic. With a smaller data set, some follow-up might be needed to compensate for missing data.

Consider the simplified example shown in Figure A1. We have a roster of some of my favorite baseball players, including their names, position, their throwing and batting orientation, along with their uniform number. Upon closer inspection, we notice that uniform numbers are missing for two of the players: Gary Gaetti and Ken Griffey. For a small problem such as this, we notice the problem immediately. For larger data sets, however, this problem

---

[11] In this context, a "record" is an individual row of a data set.

is not as obvious – we should sort our uniform numbers so that the missing values are exposed. Figure A2 details one way this can be done.

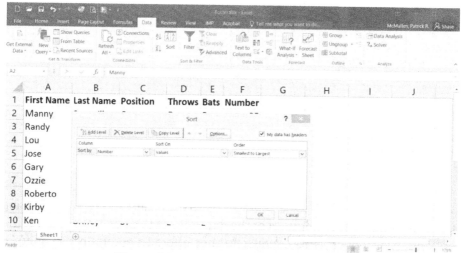

Figure A2. Sorting on Uniform Number

To expose the missing uniform numbers, we can "sort on" the uniform number. In order to do this, we first paint the entire data range, including column headings. We then select Data | Sort. We will then see a box requesting information – also shown in Figure A3. We first make certain that the box stating "My data has headers" is checked. From there, we are asked the column on which to sort – we select "Number," for uniform number. We are than asked what entity on which to sort – we select "Value." Finally, we are asked the ordering of our desired sort – we can select either here. If we select "Smallest to Largest," our missing values will be on the bottom. If we select "Largest to Smallest," our missing values will be on top. To execute the actual sort, we click the "OK" button. The sorted data set is shown in Figure A3.

Figure A3. Sorted Data Set

Figure A3 shows the sorted data set, with the observations having missing uniform numbers at the bottom of the data set. At this point, there are some options. One option is to conduct further effort to ascertain the uniform numbers of Gary Gaetti and Ken Griffey. The second option would be to delete these two rows altogether. Regardless of what approach is chosen, this process is repeated for each data field[12] until all missing items are treated.

As stated before, larger data sets with a few missing data items is likely not problematic. For smaller data sets, however missing data is more of a problem, and efforts are typically made to find the missing data values. The unfortunately reality is that missing data and "messy" data sets are the rule as opposed to the exception.

References

My knowledge of statistics has accumulated over the years to the point where most all of what has been written here has come from experience. As such, the references I cite below are from books that I like, books I have used in the past, or books in my collection that history has deemed as important.

---

[12] In this context, a "data field" is simple a column.

Albright, C., Winston, W. and Zappe, C. "Data Analysis and Decision Making, 4th Edition." Cengage Learning. Cincinnati, OH. 2011.

Bowerman, B., O'Connell, R. and Murphee, E. "Business Statistics in Practice." Irwin/McGraw-Hill. New York, New York. 2011.

Brightman, H. "Statistics in Plain English." Southwestern Publishing. Cincinnati, OH. 1986.

Gaither, N. and Frazier, G. "Operations Management." Southwestern Publishing. Cincinnati, OH. 2002.

Sharpe, N., DeVeaux, R. and Velleman, P. "Business Statistics: A First Course." Pearson Higher Education. New York, New York. 2014.

Sternstein, M. "Statistics." Barron's College Review Series. Hauppauge, New York. 1996.

Wonnacott, T.H. and Wonnatott, R.J. "Introductory Statistics." John Wiley & Sons. New York, New York. 1990.

Made in the USA
Middletown, DE
12 January 2025

69347289R00116